DAY BY DAY
THROUGH LENT

Reflections, Prayers, Practices

Daniel L. Lowery, C.SS.R.

LIGUORI
PUBLICATIONS

One Liguori Drive
Liguori, Missouri 63057
(314) 464-2500

Imprimi Potest:
John F. Dowd, C.SS.R.
Provincial, St. Louis Province
Redemptorist Fathers

Imprimatur:
Monsignor Edward J. O'Donnell
Vicar General, Archdiocese of St. Louis

ISBN 0-89243-194-6
Library of Congress Catalog Card Number: 83-82033

Cover design by Pam Hummelsheim
Cover photo by Gene Plaisted

Copyright © 1983, Liguori Publications
Printed in U.S.A.

*Dedicated to
the Redemptoristine Nuns
whose contemplative lives
inspire all of us to watch and pray.*

TABLE OF CONTENTS

FOREWORD

Lent is a special time for Christians: a time of grace, of conversion, of renewal. There are many hallowed ways of "keeping Lent." The Gospel calls us to prayer, penance, almsgiving. The Church calls us to fast and abstinence, personal and communal worship, the works of mercy. Many Catholics choose particular penances and practices of self-denial, attend daily Mass, reach out to neighbors in need.

This book grew out of my personal efforts in recent years to "keep Lent" by reflecting more seriously on the Word of God and by applying that Word to my daily life. The revised *Lectionary* of the Church offers a rich menu of biblical readings for each day of Lent. These readings highlight the major themes of the season: faith, conversion, Baptism, prayer, penance, charity.

The first reading of each day is from the Old Testament; the dominant themes are God's covenant with his people, his promise and gift of the Suffering Servant, his call to repentance and conversion. The Gospel readings for the first three weeks of Lent are chosen from Matthew, Mark, and Luke; no particular order is evident, but some of the major events in the life and ministry of Jesus (for example, his temptation in the desert, his transfiguration, his encounter with the Samaritan woman) are emphasized. Beginning with the fourth week of Lent, the challenging Gospel of John is read in order.

The purpose of DAY BY DAY THROUGH LENT is to help the reader reflect on these biblical readings, to pray over them, and to apply them to his or her own life. The format of the book is simple: After indicating the Scripture readings for the day, I focus on one passage from one of the readings. I then offer a *reflection* on that passage. In these reflections I try to throw light on the basic biblical meaning of the passage and also show how this meaning touches our lives.

(Since the readings were selected precisely for the liturgies of Lent, there is a certain amount of repetition of major themes: Baptism, for example, is emphasized frequently; so, too, are repentance and charity. But since these reflections are not meant to be read straight through, as one would read a novel, I trust that the repetition will not be too distracting.)

After the *reflection* is a *prayer,* drawn ordinarily from the Psalms or from the Liturgy and suited to the theme of the reflection. My hope is that the brief prayer cited here would be a prayer-*starter,* a point of departure for the more personal and intimate prayer of the reader.

Finally, there is a *practice:* a suggested way of applying the Word of God in a concrete fashion. It goes without saying that these suggested practices are simply examples of what an individual might do. The practice for the day will be of value in the measure that it touches one's real life.

I offer this book, then, not as a neat package but as a practical help: a help to reflect on the Word of God, a help to respond to that Word in love and prayer, a help to apply that Word to one's life and circumstances. I think of these reflections, prayers, and practices as potential *springboards* from which the reader can leap into a more intimate dialogue with the Lord and a more personal response to his Word.

I ask the Lord of Lent to bless all those people who, in various ways, have helped me to understand and appreciate the Word of God. At the same time I ask the Lord to bless all those who use this book. From those who gain something from it (and even from those who don't) I ask a small prayer for the author:

Daniel L. Lowery, C.SS.R.

ASH WEDNESDAY

Scripture Readings: Joel 2:12-17
2 Corinthians 5:20-6:2
Matthew 6:1-6,16-18

"Rend your hearts, not your garments, and return to the LORD your God" (Joel 2:13).

A MATTER OF THE HEART

Jesus clashed frequently with the Pharisees. The Pharisees were a religious sect of the Jews who originally held to very high standards of religion and morality. At the time of Jesus, however, the original spirit of the Pharisees had largely degenerated into legalism and hypocrisy (though there were still some very good people among them).

It would be rash to try to summarize in a short space all of the differences between Jesus and the Pharisees, but surely we can see that one of the greatest differences was about morality. Jesus reproached the Pharisees for their legalism, their externalism, their hardness of heart. He accused them of putting their man-made traditions and practices above the law of God (Matthew 15:1-10). He faulted them for placing heavy burdens on the shoulders of the people while not lifting a finger to help lighten the burdens (Matthew 23:4). He warned them about doing good deeds simply to attract the attention of others (Matthew 6:1-6).

In stark contrast to the morality of the Pharisees, Jesus taught a "morality of the heart." He was concerned about the interior dispositions of the mind and will. To Jesus the internal motive from which an action springs is more important than the external act itself. In a strong passage in the Gospel of Matthew, Jesus spells out his theme in clear and down-to-earth terms:

"He called the people to him and said, 'Listen, and understand. What goes into the mouth does not make a man unclean; it is what comes out of the mouth that makes him unclean. . . . Can you not

11

see that whatever goes into the mouth passes through the stomach and is discharged . . . ? But the things that come out of the mouth come from the heart, and it is these that make a man unclean. For from the heart come evil intentions: murder, adultery, fornication, theft, perjury, slander. These are the things that make a man unclean'' (Matthew 15:11-20, *The Jerusalem Bible*).

This teaching of Jesus challenges all of us, for there is a bit of the Pharisee in the best of us. We are challenged to ask ourselves certain questions: If I fail to keep the law of God, do I understand that I must look first at my heart to know why, not merely at my actions? Do I keep the law of God only in an external, face-saving way? Or does my obedience come from the heart?

The commandments are broken first in our hearts. Murder (anger, violence) is an external act, but it begins in the profound depth of our hearts where hatred and disrespect and resentment reside unchecked. Adultery is committed spiritually before it is committed physically. The external words used to lie or ruin the good name of others are conceived in an ugly heart.

The cry of the prophet Joel, which the Church uses to open this season of Lent, is: ''Rend your hearts, not your garments'' (Joel 2:13). The external acts of penance such as fasting and almsgiving must touch our hearts, not merely our external behavior. Conversion, like morality, is a matter of the heart. We cannot change our conduct unless we first change our hearts.

Saint John, at the end of the second chapter of his Gospel, says that Jesus ''needed no one to give him testimony about human nature. He was well aware of what was in man's heart'' (John 2:25). The true Christian is one who never forgets that truth.

PRAYER: ''A clean heart create for me, O God,
        and a steadfast spirit renew within me''
    (Psalm 51:12).

PRACTICE: I will fast today for the glory of God and in solidarity with the hungry of the world.

THURSDAY AFTER ASH WEDNESDAY
Scripture Readings: Deuteronomy 30:15-20
Luke 9:22-25
"Whoever wishes to be my follower must deny his very self, take up his cross each day, and follow in my steps" (Luke 9:23).

THE SIGN OF THE CROSS

Like pebbles on a beach, suffering is part of the human landscape. And, like pebbles, suffering comes in different shapes and sizes. There is physical suffering: not only the aches and pains of daily life but also the serious illnesses that can come upon us in the blinking of an eye. There is emotional suffering: the loneliness, depression, or fear that bedevil so many lives. There is spiritual suffering: the desire to overcome temptation, the intention to grow in holiness — and the failure to do so.

Each of us could easily pinpoint the suffering that most severely touches our lives. With a little reflection we could also name the chief suffering of our family members, our relatives, our friends. From experience, we know that everybody suffers in one way or another. Suffering plays no favorites. The religious person suffers; so does the atheist.

The key question that confronts us, then, is not *whether* we will suffer but *how* we will suffer. How are we to deal with suffering? Throughout history, people have sought a solution to suffering. There are many philosophies and many schools of thought. The Stoics, for example, insisted on an attitude of endurance in the face of pain, a refusal to acknowledge suffering or give in to complaint. The Buddhists, on the other hand, said that the best approach was to suppress all desire, experience nirvana or oblivion. If you desire nothing, you cannot be hurt or disappointed.

The Christian view, in most simple terms, is acceptance of

suffering in union with Christ. The sufferings of Christ were redemptive because they were enriched with love. "In thinking of the passion of Jesus," writes Saint Alphonsus, "we should consider not so much the sorrows Jesus suffered as the love with which he bore them."

A disciple of Jesus must have the same attitude toward suffering that Jesus had. "Whoever wishes to be my follower must deny his very self, take up his cross each day, and follow in my steps." If our sufferings are united with the sufferings of Christ, if they are motivated by love, then they too can be redemptive. Suffering can be wasted; it can lead to bitterness. But suffering can also lead to a higher level of unselfish love.

When I was a boy it was said, half-jokingly, that there was no use telling your troubles to a priest or a nun because they would tell you only one thing: Offer it up! While this advice may have been overused at times, and used to oversimplify, it is still good advice. To offer up our sufferings in union with Christ is a basic message of the Gospel. In our sufferings we join with Jesus in the ongoing work of redemption. Instead of letting our sufferings make us bitter or hardhearted, we offer them with compassion and love in union with him.

There are plenty of opportunities in daily life to offer up our sufferings in union with Christ. During Lent, especially, we might take another look at the cross that casts its shadow over our lives: the nagging headache, the chronic illness, the stifling boredom, the vague discouragement, the moody loneliness, the spiritual emptiness. Let us take that cross and unite it with the Cross of Christ. And let us do so not grudgingly but lovingly.

PRAYER: "We adore you, O Christ, and we praise you, because by your holy cross you have redeemed the world" (Good Friday Liturgy).

PRACTICE: Today I will unite this particular cross of mine *(name it)* with the sufferings of Jesus.

FRIDAY AFTER ASH WEDNESDAY
Scripture Readings: Isaiah 58:1-9
Matthew 9:14-15
"Do you call this a fast,
a day acceptable to the LORD?"
(Isaiah 58:5)

WHAT KIND OF FAST?

Fasting has a long history among religious people. It has always been a way of expiating sin, a way of purifying the spirit, a way of offering up something to the Lord. In the Christian tradition, too, fasting has held an honored place. At the same time, however, the spiritual masters have been a bit wary of fasting because of the Lord's warning in Matthew: "When you fast you are not to look glum as the hypocrites do. They change the appearance of their faces so that others may see they are fasting. I assure you, they are already repaid" (Matthew 6:16). There is a subtle temptation to make of fasting a vain display of virtue. It seems uncommonly difficult for a Christian to fast without making a display of it or without looking down his nose at those poor unfortunates who do not have enough willpower to fast!

The first reading of today emphasizes another point about fasting, one that pious people seem often to forget. Isaiah links fasting and social justice.

"Is this the manner of fasting I wish,
of keeping a day of penance:
That a man bow his head like a reed,
and lie in sackcloth and ashes?
Do you call this a fast,
a day acceptable to the LORD?
This, rather, is the fasting I wish:
releasing those bound unjustly,
untying the thongs of the yoke,

15

Setting free the oppressed,
　breaking every yoke;
Sharing your bread with the hungry,
　sheltering the oppressed and the homeless;
Clothing the naked when you see them,
　and not turning your back on your own'' (Isaiah 58:5-7).

These haunting words of Isaiah remind us of the powerful portrait of the Last Judgment painted by Jesus: ''The king will say to those on his right: 'Come. You have my Father's blessing. . . . For I was hungry and you gave me food, I was thirsty and you gave me drink. I was a stranger and you welcomed me, naked and you clothed me. I was ill and you comforted me, in prison and you came to visit me . . . ' '' (Matthew 25:34-36). Jesus would not allow a false piety to dominate the hearts of his disciples.

Saint James, in his turn, spells out the practical implications of a false piety. ''My brothers, what good is it to profess faith without practicing it? Such faith has no power to save one, has it? If a brother or sister has nothing to wear and no food for the day, and you say to them, 'Good-bye and good luck! Keep warm and well fed,' but do not meet their bodily needs, what good is that? So it is with the faith that does nothing in practice. It is thoroughly lifeless'' (James 2:14-17).

Traditionally, Lenten practices have emphasized fasting and prayer. This is as it should be, because in these ways we can honor the Lord and grow in the spirit. But the ''almsgiving'' of the Gospel — the practice of charity and justice — must not be neglected. Lent challenges us, first of all, to Gospel simplicity: to right priorities and a simpler life-style. The poor cannot fast because they have nothing to eat. Those who are well-off must look for ways of sharing with the poor. While it is true that there are family and social obligations which cannot be lightly dismissed, it is also true that many of us have more than we need or can ever responsibly use. The Christ whom we love and serve was born poor, lived a poor life, identified with the poor, and died poor. We can hardly consider ourselves his disciples if the poor find no place in our hearts.

PRAYER: "Hear my prayer, O LORD;
to my cry give ear;
to my weeping be not deaf!
For I am but a wayfarer before you,
a pilgrim like all my fathers" (Psalm 39:13).

PRACTICE: I will fast today and will give the money saved to the poor.

SATURDAY AFTER ASH WEDNESDAY
Scripture Readings: Isaiah 58:9-14
Luke 5:27-32
"I have not come to invite the self-righteous to a change of heart, but sinners" (Luke 5:32).

THE CALL TO CONVERSION

The call to conversion is the most frequent and most radical call of the New Testament. The Greek word is *metanoia,* usually translated as "conversion" or "repentance." It means something very profound, very personal, very pervasive. It signifies not merely a change of manners but a change of heart. It implies a total transformation of oneself, complete conformity to the will of the Father. (See Matthew 7:21-23.) It means allowing our attitudes, values, life-style to be judged by the word of God. It means submitting our personalities and priorities to the penetrating light of that word.

There is a negative aspect to conversion. It involves a turning away from sin. It is not possible to understand the call to conversion without understanding the significance of sin. The Lenten liturgies are meaningless if sin is reduced to mere psychological limitation or legalistic failing. Jesus makes a sharp distinction between the self-righteous and the sinful. Only those who recognize themselves as sinners can receive the grace of conversion. This means that we must not only acknowledge our sinful acts but also the sinful roots of them: the inner attitudes and dispositions that are estranged from God.

There is also a positive aspect to conversion. It is always a kind of homecoming, a return to the Father's love. That is why the parable of the Prodigal Son is considered one of the greatest conversion stories of the Bible. There is nothing abstract or academic about conversion. It is a movement toward love, a renewed personal intimacy and friendship with God. It is a return to the Father's arms. Conversion celebrates the victory of light over darkness, good over evil, life over death. It is a cause of joy in heaven (Luke 15:7) and a sign of hope on earth.

Conversion is a grace, a gift of the Lord. It is not possible for us to achieve it on our own. While it is true that conversion ultimately demands our free consent and cooperation, we are powerless to achieve it by ourselves. The gentle invitation of Jesus is effective. It enables us to hear his call and to respond to it. The love of Christ forgives, heals, renews, strengthens. The grace of Christ is stronger than our weakness or sinfulness. "My grace is enough for you, for in weakness power reaches perfection" (2 Corinthians 12:9).

Conversion is not an isolated act but an ongoing process. The 1973 Decree on the new Rite of Reconciliation expresses this very well: "The people of God accomplishes and perfects this continual repentance in many different ways. It shares in the sufferings of Christ by enduring its own difficulties, carries out works of mercy and charity, and adopts ever more fully the outlook of the Gospel message. Thus the people of God becomes in the world a sign of conversion to God. All this the Church expresses in its life and celebrates in the liturgy when the faithful confess that they are sinners and ask pardon of God and of their brothers and sisters. This happens in penitential services, in the proclamation of the word of God, in prayer, and in the penitential aspects of the eucharistic celebration. In the sacrament of penance the faithful obtain from the mercy of God pardon for their sins against him; at the same time they are reconciled with the Church which they wounded by their sins and which works for their conversion by charity, example, and prayer.''

PRAYER: ''You are my God; have pity on me,
   O Lord,
  for to you I call all the day.
Gladden the soul of your servant,
  for to you, O Lord, I lift up my soul'' (Psalm 86:3-4).

PRACTICE: Today I will prepare for a Lenten celebration of the sacrament of reconciliation.

FIRST SUNDAY OF LENT

Scripture Readings: Cycle A
                            Genesis 2:7-9, 3:1-7
                            Romans 5:12-19
                            Matthew 4:1-11

                            Cycle B
                            Genesis 9:8-15
                            1 Peter 3:18-22
                            Mark 1:12-15

                            Cycle C
                            Deuteronomy 26:4-10
                            Romans 10:8-13
                            Luke 4:1-13

(Note: The following reflection, TEMPTATION, is suitable for Cycle A, B, or C.)

FIRST SUNDAY OF LENT
Scripture Readings: Cycle A, B, C
"Jesus was led into the desert by the Spirit to be tempted by the devil" (Matthew 4:1).

TEMPTATION

In a way, it is reassuring to know that Jesus was subject to temptation. It somehow emphasizes his humanity; for, though we know by faith that he is truly man as well as truly God, do not most of us hesitate to think of him as really human? It is true, of course, as both Matthew and Luke emphasize, that he was "led by the Spirit" and "filled with the Spirit" during his lonely ordeal. Yet, he did experience a struggle; he had to reaffirm his complete acceptance of the Father's will.

The three temptations essentially invite Jesus to be a false Messiah. He is urged to be a political Messiah, a powerful Ruler. He is asked to consider the human privileges of wealth and glory and power that would naturally follow upon a political Messiahship. The truth is that many of the Jews were expecting such a Messiah anyway. Why not take advantage of their expectations?

Jesus, showing his familiarity with the Old Testament, sternly refuses the attractive propositions offered by Satan. He chooses instead complete dependence on God, a recognition that God and his will must always come first, a willingness to obey God at any cost. In effect, Jesus states that nothing — not pleasure, not power, not wealth — must ever come between us and the saving will of God.

The temptations which Jesus faced are experienced anew, in a thousand disguises, by the individual Christian and by the community of the Church. There is the ever-present temptation to bring God down to our level rather than to reach up to his. There is a temptation to see prayer as a bargaining power, to view faith as an insurance policy, to prize religion for the respectability it gives.

There is the even more subtle temptation, as Saint Augustine said, to make God in our own image and likeness and, while mouthing pieties, to trust only in ourselves.

The first reading from Genesis (3:1-7) describes in rich imagery the psychology of temptation. Have we not had similar experiences? There is a perverse desire in human nature to "fool around" with temptation, even though one may genuinely not want to fall. The woman Eve "saw that the tree was good for food, pleasing to the eyes, and desirable for gaining wisdom." By that time, not surprisingly, she was trapped; and she fell into grave disobedience against God.

The greatest lesson we learn from Jesus is his steadfast obedience to the Father's will. Jesus did not "fool around" with temptation. He knew what the Scriptures had said; he understood his vocation. Without hesitation, he reaffirmed his fidelity to God. Though we have been admonished from youth to respond quickly in the face of temptation, do we not find ourselves taking chances and delaying action? While on one level of our being we want to be faithful, on another level do we not also want to experience the glamour and excitement of being tempted?

The stance of Jesus in the desert teaches us, the pilgrim People of God, that we too must live by the Word of God, not presume to challenge God's promises, and serve God alone. Meanwhile, amid the temptations and struggles of life, we should always remember that "God keeps his promises. He will not let you be tested beyond your strength. Along with the test he will give you a way out of it so that you may be able to endure it" (1 Corinthians 10:13).

PRAYER: "Have mercy on me, O God, in your goodness. . . .
Thoroughly wash me from my guilt
and of my sin cleanse me" (Psalm 51:3-4).

PRACTICE: I will try to deal with this temptation *(name it)* in accord with the spirit of Jesus.

MONDAY, FIRST WEEK OF LENT
Scripture Readings: Leviticus 19:1-2,11-18
Matthew 25:35-46
"Be holy, for I, the LORD, your God, am holy" (Leviticus 19:2).

THE HOLINESS OF GOD

The Book of Leviticus is sometimes referred to as the book of holiness. It frequently highlights the transcendent holiness of God, the source of all holiness, a holiness which we, in our turn, are called to imitate. There is an ever-present, yet subtle, temptation to think of holiness in terms of ritual performance or human perfectionism. Do not many of us actually believe that holiness depends mostly on us, on our moral life, our practice of virtue?

This emphasis is clearly misplaced. The truth is that holiness belongs essentially to God, "the fountain of all holiness." Our holiness is not something devised by us, but is in truth a sharing in the holiness of God. Echoing Leviticus, Saint Peter writes: " . . . become holy yourselves in every aspect of your conduct, after the likeness of the holy One who called you . . ." (1 Peter 1:15).

Holiness is the fruit of God's covenant with us. This covenant was effected not by any human efforts but by the gracious love of God for us, made visible in his only Son. "Realize that you were delivered from the futile way of life your fathers handed on to you, not by any diminishable sum of silver or gold, but by Christ's blood beyond all price: the blood of a spotless, unblemished lamb chosen before the world's foundation and revealed for your sake in these last days" (1 Peter 1:18-20).

The misguided tendency to feature human effort over divine grace is frequently challenged by New Testament writers. In his letter to Titus, Saint Paul affirms: "But when the kindness and

23

love of God our Savior appeared, he saved us; not because of any righteous deeds we had done, but because of his mercy" (Titus 3:4-5). Human efforts are useless without the grace of God and rebirth by the Holy Spirit.

The first letter to the Johannine community emphasizes the same truth.

"God's love for us was revealed when God
sent his only Son to the world
that we might have life through him.
Love, then, consists in this:
not that we have loved God
but that he has loved us
and has sent his Son as an offering for our sins" (1 John 4:9-10).
Holiness begins not with us but with God's free initiative of love, which reaches its high point in the sending of his beloved Son in expiation for our sins.

Is not the teaching of these Scripture passages that we are sanctified (made holy) because of the mercy and love of God freely given to us, not because of our righteous deeds or because of our efforts to love God first? This emphasis, this perspective, is not only theologically correct but also extremely practical for us. If we put the emphasis on our own good actions, we will easily become discouraged. If we believe that God's love and mercy are dependent on our righteous actions, we may easily doubt his love and mercy.

Does it follow, then, that we need not worry about our actions, about how we live or what we do? Not at all! As disciples of Jesus, we are called to do the Father's will, to live according to the law of love, to abide by the teachings of the Church. To be sure, we have a part to play in holiness; today's Gospel reading is eloquent testimony to that. We are called to respond to God's gracious love by living a fervent Christian life. What we want to remember, however, is that our part is secondary. It is not nearly as important as God's part!

PRAYER: "O LORD, hear my prayer. . . .
And enter not into judgment with your servant,
for before you no living man is just" (Psalm 143:1-2).

PRACTICE: Today I will give special thanks to God for his gracious kindness to me and to all his people.

TUESDAY, FIRST WEEK OF LENT
Scripture Readings: Isaiah 55:10-11
Matthew 6:7-15
"This is how you are to pray . . . " (Matthew 6:9).

THE LORD'S PRAYER

We know the prayer by heart and say it often. It is perhaps the best-known prayer in the world. It is a precious prayer because it comes to us from Jesus himself: the Lord's prayer, the "Our Father." Through the centuries many of the saints have written explicit meditations on this prayer, taking apart the words, as it were, so that their meaning could take deep roots in their hearts. The reflections which follow are basically those of Saint Cyprian who wrote them around A.D. 250.

Our Father, who art in heaven: One of the greatest truths of our faith is that we are the adopted sons and daughters of God and so can call him Father. "To his own he came, yet his own did not accept him. Any who did accept him he empowered to become children of God" (John 1:11-12). It is noteworthy that we are not instructed to say "my Father," for we do not pray for ourselves alone, but we pray as members of the community of the Church, the sons and daughters of God, and we pray for the good of all.

Hallowed be thy name: It is not as if we think we make God holy by our prayers. Rather, we are asking that his name may be made holy in us. We pray that we who have been hallowed (made holy) in Baptism may persevere in what we have begun.

Thy kingdom come: We pray that God's kingdom will become present for us in the same way that we ask for his name to be hallowed among us. We pray that the kingdom built for us by God, the kingdom won by the death and Resurrection of Christ, will fully come. And we plead that we who were formerly slaves will be living members of that kingdom.

Thy will be done on earth as it is in heaven: Our prayer here is that we may carry out God's saving will in our lives. All that Jesus did and all that he taught was "the will of God." We pray that in the face of obstacles and temptations we may have help and strength to do his will.

Give us this day our daily bread: This petition may be understood in a spiritual and in a literal way. Spiritually, Christ himself is our bread of life; he is our "food for the journey." In addition, we believe that our Father knows our needs, and we trust that he will take care of us. We pray that his loving providence may envelop us.

And forgive us our trespasses: We acknowledge that we are indeed sinners, that each day finds us unfaithful in this way or that. But we also recognize our Father's great love, mercy, forgiveness. We believe that our Father truly forgives our sins.

As we forgive those who trespass against us: Jesus clearly laid down a condition for our forgiveness — namely, that our debts be forgiven insofar as we forgive our debtors. How many parables and sayings of Jesus emphasize this truth! If we hope for forgiveness from God, we must be ready to forgive others.

And lead us not into temptation: Here we pray not out of fear that God himself will lead us astray but, rather, to show our confidence that God can give us an escape from temptation and that "he will not let you be tested beyond your strength" (1 Corinthians 10:13).

But deliver us from evil: We pray to be kept safe from the power of Satan, the Evil One, and all that he stands for. We pray that God will overcome evil in our lives.

PRAYER: "Father, Lord of heaven and earth, to you I offer praise; for what you have hidden from the learned and the clever, you have revealed to the merest children" (Matthew 11:25).

PRACTICE: Today *(every day)* I will pray this prayer of Jesus with special attention.

WEDNESDAY, FIRST WEEK OF LENT
Scripture Readings: Jonah 3:1-10
Luke 11:29-32
"Just as Jonah was a sign for the Ninevites, so will the Son of Man be a sign for the present age" (Luke 11:30).

THE SIGN OF JONAH

The story of Jonah is a marvelous (and humorous) example of the give-and-take between the Lord and his prophets. At the same time, it reveals a religious message of universal application. Jonah was a reluctant prophet. In fact, he ran away from his divine commission. While trying to escape by ship, he was cast over-board and was taken into the belly of a great fish for three days. Finally rescued, he was ready to do what God wanted him to do. He traveled from Palestine to Nineveh to preach repentance to the people there. Yet, in a narrow spirit of vindictiveness, he hoped that the people would not repent! He wanted to see them destroyed.

Despite Jonah's pessimism, however, the people were open to his preaching. Every citizen, from the least to the greatest, fasted and repented of his or her sins. God responded kindly to their repentance. "When God saw by their actions how they turned away from their evil way, he repented of the evil that he had threatened to do to them; he did not carry it out" (Jonah 3:10).

It is not often that Jesus gives a direct commentary on the Old Testament. In today's passage from the Gospel of Luke, however, Jesus explains that Jonah was a sign to the Ninevites. Here the term "sign" refers not to the kind of miracle many of his listeners were demanding but, rather, to a notable or paradoxical event manifesting the presence and activity of God. Jonah was a sign, a manifestation of the power and grace of God among the sinful Ninevites.

Jesus then goes on to point out that just as Jonah was a sign to the Ninevites, so is Jesus himself ("the Son of Man" and "greater than Jonah") a sign to his listeners. But unlike the Ninevites, the people of this "present generation" to whom Jesus preached did not repent. And so "at the judgment, the citizens of Nineveh will rise along with the present generation, and they will condemn it" (Luke 11:32).

The primitive Christian community saw a marvelous resemblance between what happened to Jonah and what happened to Jesus. "Just as Jonah spent three days and three nights in the belly of the whale, so will the Son of Man spend three days and three nights in the bowels of the earth" (Matthew 12:40). By his generous obedience to the Father's will ("becoming obedient to death, even the death of the cross") and by his glorious Resurrection at the hands of the Father, Jesus is now the only sign we need. He summons us, as Jonah did the Ninevites, to repent and to be open to God's redeeming love. Jesus is indeed more than a sign: he is the reality of God's saving presence and activity among us.

A few years ago I participated in a high school retreat at the beginning of Lent. Before the liturgy of the day, the students paraded around the gym with homemade banners. One of the banners said: "Repent in Lent!" It was a shorthand way of saying what Jonah said to the Ninevites and what Jesus says to us. It is both an ancient message and an urgent one. Now is the time for us to take it seriously.

PRAYER: "Remember that your compassion, O LORD,
               and your kindness are from of old.
               The sins of my youth and my frailties
                  remember not;
               in your kindness remember me, because of your
               goodness, O LORD" (Psalm 25:6)

PRACTICE: Today I will spend five minutes in calm prayer,
               repenting all the sins of my life.

THURSDAY, FIRST WEEK OF LENT
**Scripture Readings: Esther, Chapter C, 12, 14-16,
                      23-25
                      Matthew 7:7-12**
**"Ask, and you will receive. Seek, and you will find.
Knock, and it will be opened to you" (Matthew 7:7).**

THE PRAYER OF PETITION

Few sayings of Jesus are as well known as the above from the Gospel of Matthew. For every human person who struggles and suffers, these encouraging words of Jesus are like a cool ointment on a painful sore. They remind us that our humble and persevering prayers are not in vain, that because of God's gracious generosity our prayers are listened to and answered.

From time to time a certain kind of elite voice is raised in the Church admonishing us not to be so hung up on "the prayer of petition," not to have the "gimme" mentality in our relationship with God. Without doubt, our spirit of prayer should include praise and adoration of the all-holy God and thanksgiving for his countless blessings. Yet, no matter how far we progress in the Christian life, there will always be a need to present our petitions before God. How privileged we are! Saint Alphonsus Liguori reminds us that "the kings of this world give audiences a few times a year but God gives us a continual audience."

Almost every Christian wonders at times about the prayer of petition. What does the promise of Jesus really mean? Why are our prayers not always answered? What are we doing wrong? It is evident that such questions arose very early in the Christian community. Saint James, for example, whose practical Epistle was written certainly before the end of the first century, addresses some of them.

Saint James tells his community: "You do not obtain because you do not ask. You ask and you do not receive because you ask wrongly, with a view to squandering what you receive on your pleasures" (James 4:2-3). It is obviously possible for us to ask for the wrong things! In the fifth century the great Saint Augustine (who knew from painful experience about asking for the wrong things) said that God will infallibly grant what is for our essential good, our eternal beatitude. But when we pray for what is opposed to this happiness, for what cannot bring it about, God mercifully refuses our prayer.

Saint Augustine reminds us that right after the "ask, and you will receive" passage of Matthew there is another which says: "Would one of you hand his son a stone when he asks for a loaf, or a poisonous snake when he asks for a fish?" (Matthew 7:9-10) If, in other words, we can trust an earthly father to give only what is good to his children, can we not trust our heavenly Father to give only good things to us? "If you, with all your sins, know how to give your children what is good, how much more will your heavenly Father give good things to anyone who asks him!'' (7:11)

The Gospel of Luke draws attention to another aspect of the prayer of petition: that is, perseverance. ''He told them a parable on the necessity of praying always and not losing heart'' (Luke 18:1). In this parable the reluctant judge yields to the widow's request because she was wearing him out with her requests! ''Will not God then do justice to his chosen who call out to him day and night?'' (Luke 18:7) With great insight Saint Augustine writes: ''Perhaps your prayers are not heard because you have ceased asking.''

Part of the intriguing story of Esther is told in the first reading of today's liturgy. Though the vindictiveness of this story is somewhat baffling to us, the example of Esther's prayer is heartening. Her prayer was made at a time when her faith was being profoundly tested. ''Save us by your power, and help me, who am alone and have no one but you, O LORD . . . '' (Esther Chapter C:25).

PRAYER: ''For you have made great above all things
  your name and your promise.
  When I called, you answered me;
  you built up strength within me'' (Psalm 138:2).

PRACTICE: I will approach the prayer of petition with a new spirit of confidence and perseverance.

Scripture Readings: Ezekiel 18:21-28
Matthew 5:20-26
"If you bring your gift to the altar and there recall that your brother has anything against you, leave your gift at the altar, go first to be reconciled with your brother, and then come and offer your gift" (Matthew 5:23-24).

THE NEW LAW OF JESUS

The disciples were waiting for Jesus. Finally, he came. He went up the hillside and began to speak to them. How fortunate they were! They heard Jesus preach the Sermon on the Mount.

Certainly, they were fortunate; but they were also probably a little confused and maybe even shocked. Jesus told them that he came not to abolish the law and the prophets but to fulfill them. This implied, of course, that the old law (the one they knew and loved) was unfinished, incomplete. It would find its completion in Jesus.

In his picturesque way of preaching, Jesus not only declares a principle but also gives six concrete examples of how the old law is to be fulfilled. One of the examples (featured in today's Gospel) concerns the commandment which forbids murder. Jesus declares that the new law forbids not only murder but also the anger which is the root of murder. Then he goes on to forbid abusive language, which is nothing more than an outward expression of the inner anger. Clearly, Jesus does not abolish the law against murder. He simply demands much more: a moral integrity and holiness which "surpasses that of the scribes and Pharisees."

At the same time the preaching of Jesus is supremely realistic. He seems to assume that people, despite their moral efforts, will at times yield to anger. What then? Then follows the sacred duty of reconciliation! "If you bring your gift to the altar and there recall that your brother has anything against you, leave your gift at the altar, go first to be reconciled with your brother, and then come and offer your gift.'' As startling as this statement is to us, it was no doubt even more startling to those who were listening to Jesus. Worship was for them the most sacred duty. But Jesus is saying that even worship must be postponed for reconciliation!

The Sermon on the Mount no doubt posed serious questions for people who first listened to it. It poses serious questions for us, too. It certainly challenges the moral minimalism which so many of us espouse. Why is it still so easy for us to spin out our legalisms and excuses that water down the new law of love? How can we pride ourselves on being disciples of Jesus when we so frequently and so casually accept moral ideals and norms that fall so short of his?

Moreover, it challenges our worship. The Eucharist is the sign and pledge of Christ's love for us. The Eucharist is a call to renewed love within the community of believers. The Eucharist demands the spirit of forgiveness, the desire for reconciliation, the sign of peace. There can be no complete Eucharistic worship if our hearts remain cold and closed to our brothers and sisters.

As it was with the scribes and Pharisees, so it is with us: It is not our human weakness that keeps us from the Lord; it is our pride, our arrogance, our coldness. The ease with which we rationalize our lack of love may, in the final analysis, be what keeps the Sermon on the Mount from penetrating our hearts.

PRAYER: "If you, O LORD, mark iniquities,
LORD, who can stand?
But with you is forgiveness,
that you may be revered" (Psalm 130:3-4).

PRACTICE: Today I will forgive from my heart all who have hurt me in any way.

SATURDAY, FIRST WEEK OF LENT
Scripture Readings: Deuteronomy 26:16-19
Matthew 5:43-48
"My command to you is: love your enemies, pray for your persecutors" (Matthew 5:44).

"LOVE YOUR ENEMIES"

In the Old Testament as in the New, love of one's neighbor was a fundamental commandment. "You shall not bear hatred for your brother in your heart. . . . Take no revenge and cherish no grudge against your fellow countrymen. You shall love your neighbor as yourself" (Leviticus 19:17-18). The neighbor is a member of one's family, town, tribe, or nation. The neighbor is one with whom a person has some natural bond or connection.

While repeating this commandment, Jesus implies that its observance is not exactly worthy of extravagant praise. "If you love those who love you, what merit is there in that? Do not tax collectors do as much?" (Matthew 5:46) Jesus demands more. "My command to you is: love your enemies, pray for your persecutors." The love of one's enemies thus becomes a distinguishing mark of authentic Christian morality. Prince Andrey (in Leo Tolstoy's *War and Peace)* gives the reason: "Someone dear to one can be loved with human love; but an enemy can only be loved with divine love."

In a land where farming was featured and the weather constantly watched, Jesus uses an analogy which everyone could grasp. Referring to the love of enemies, he says: "This will prove that you are sons of the heavenly Father, for his sun rises on the bad and the good, he rains on the just and the unjust" (Matthew 5:45).

Commenting on this text, Father John McKenzie summarizes: "Here Jesus presents God's attitude toward men as the model of the Christian's attitude toward those who hate him. Love of one's neighbor is a general and regular attitude which the Christian exhibits, and it is no more dependent upon the behavior of one's neighbor than is the course of nature, which God maintains for sinners as well as for the righteous . . ." *(Dictionary of the Bible)*.

But who is my enemy? The parable of the Good Samaritan gives a clue. The hostility between the Jews and the Samaritans was deep. By telling the parable, Jesus was indicating that the Jews must love even those from whom they felt most estranged (see Luke 10:29-37). Does this not include, for me too, those of other races, strange creeds, foreign cultures? Does it not include those whose philosophy of life and style of living are at odds with mine? Does it not include those who are "strange," those who march to a different drummer?

And who is my persecutor? Is it not the person who speaks kindly to my face but harshly behind my back? Is it not the one who uses my friendship for base motives? The one who jealously tears down the good I have tried to do? The one who slyly insults me, puts me down, corrects me, passes over me? Are not these, and others like them, the people for whom I should be praying?

Martin Luther King, who knew a fair amount about enemies and persecutors, was once asked if he had ever met a true Christian — that is, one who actually loved his enemies. Dr. King is said to have responded: "I have met many such Christians. It is their example that makes me want to be one of them." In truth, he became one of them. His example could strengthen our desire to be one of them too.

But the ultimate example is Jesus himself. For those who persecuted him even unto death, his gentle love could express itself in prayer: "Father, forgive them; they do not know what they are doing" (Luke 23:34).

PRAYER: "You have commanded that your precepts
be diligently kept.
Oh, that I might be firm in the ways
of keeping your statutes!" (Psalm 119:4-5)

PRACTICE: Today I will treat with charity a particular person *(name him or her)* who is in some way an enemy to me.

SECOND SUNDAY OF LENT

Scripture Readings: Cycle A
　　　　　　　　　Genesis 12:1-4
　　　　　　　　　2 Timothy 1:8-10
　　　　　　　　　Matthew 17:1-9

　　　　　　　　　Cycle B
　　　　　　　　　Genesis 22:1-2,9,10-13,15-18
　　　　　　　　　Romans 8:31-34
　　　　　　　　　Mark 9:2-10

　　　　　　　　　Cycle C
　　　　　　　　　Genesis 15:5-12,17-18
　　　　　　　　　Philippians 3:17 — 4:1
　　　　　　　　　Luke 9:28-36

(Note: The following Reflection, TRANSFIGURATION, is suitable for Cycle A, B, or C.)

SECOND SUNDAY OF LENT
Scripture Readings: Cycle A, B, C
"He was transfigured before their eyes" (Matthew 17:2).

TRANSFIGURATION

The Italian artist, Raphael, who was only thirty-seven when he died, managed to produce a large number of excellent religious paintings. One of his most famous is entitled "Transfiguration." The painting is done, as it were, on two levels. The first level, at the top of the canvas, shows Jesus raised up in a billow of clouds, his garment dazzling and his face radiant — as if his divine nature is shining through his human nature. On the right is Moses holding the Law. On the left is Elijah, the prophet. At the feet of Jesus, awestruck and reverent, are the apostles Peter, James, and John.

The second level of the painting is dark and somber. We see a young boy standing by a cot, surrounded by his family and by the disciples of Jesus. The boy is obviously afflicted, suffering. Two disciples are especially noticeable: One is pointing to the afflicted child; the other is pointing toward Jesus. The message seems to be: "Yes, this boy is afflicted and troubled. He must look to Jesus for strength."

With some artistic license, this painting communicates the profound meaning of the Transfiguration. There is no doubt that the Transfiguration was a moment of glory for Jesus and of light for his disciples. Surprisingly, however, even in the midst of the glory and light, the Transfiguration scene is linked with the suffering and death of Jesus and the doctrine of the cross for his followers.

Shortly before the Transfiguration event, Jesus reminds his disciples that "the Son of Man . . . must first endure many sufferings, be rejected by the elders, the high priests and the scribes, and be put to death, and then be raised up on the third day"

(Luke 9:22). At that time he announced the doctrine of the cross: "If a man wishes to come after me, he must deny his very self, take up his cross, and begin to follow in my footsteps" (Matthew 16:24). Even at the time of the Transfiguration itself, "They . . . spoke of his passage, which he was about to fulfill in Jerusalem" (Luke 9:31).

The Transfiguration event beautifully reminded the disciples of the glory Jesus possessed and that his glory would ultimately overcome the darkness of evil in his life and in theirs. But the glory would come later. First would come the cross.

There is no way to be a disciple of Jesus without the cross. The cross, to be sure, takes many forms. But it is always present. What is the cross in my life at this time? Perhaps it is one of the ordinary crosses of daily living: the headaches and heartaches, the boredom of school or work, the frustration of rubbing elbows with many different kinds of people. Or perhaps it is the much heavier cross of serious illness, chronic pain, agonizing depression, nagging fear, relentless temptation.

Whatever the cross, the way to carry it is in union with Christ. His Cross is the symbol of redemption. Our crosses, too, must be redemptive. They can be if they are joined to his. Like the boy in Raphael's painting, we must look to Jesus for the true meaning of the cross and for the strength to bear it.

In its deepest meaning, the Transfiguration underlines the glorious truth as proclaimed by Paul: "If we have died with Christ, we believe that we are also to live with him" (Romans 6:8).

PRAYER: "Our soul waits for the LORD,
               who is our help and our shield. . . .
             May your kindness, O LORD, be upon us
               who have put our hope in you" (Psalm 33:20).

PRACTICE: Today I will unite this particular cross *(name it)*
             with the suffering of Christ.

MONDAY, SECOND WEEK OF LENT
Scripture Readings: Daniel 9:4-10
Luke 6:36-38
"Be compassionate, as your heavenly Father is compassionate" (Luke 6:36).

COMPASSION

If the Gospel of Luke had to be given a single title, it could be called "Compassion." The perfection of God, as described by Luke, consists in compassion. The Father is the Compassionate One, the one who is "rich in mercy" (Ephesians 2:4). Jesus is the visible and living sign of the Father's compassion. "Not only does he speak of it and explain it by the use of comparisons and parables," writes Pope John Paul II, "but above all he himself makes it incarnate and personifies it" *(Rich in Mercy)*. The disciple of Jesus, too, is called to imitate the compassion of God.

Compassion comes from two Latin words meaning to "suffer with." (The word "sympathy" is the Greek equivalent.) The dictionary defines compassion as "sympathetic consciousness of others' distress together with a desire to alleviate it." Thus compassion includes both entering into the pain of another and also wanting to do something about it.

Both of these elements are underscored in the insightful description of compassion by William McKee, C.SS.R.: "Compassion is a virtue with many faces. It is a sharing of pain or failure or brokenness or fear or anxiety. It sometimes means to mourn with those who mourn, to be lonely with those who are lonely, to be weak with those who are weak . . . . The compassionate are not in the lifeboat throwing life preservers to those drowning in the ocean; they are in the ocean themselves, helping the others into the boat or to the safety of the shore" *(Liguorian,* March 1983).

To imitate the compassion of God means to imitate his way of judging and acting. This imitation involves, on the negative side, not judging or condemning our neighbor and, on the positive side, forgiveness and generosity. "Do not judge, and you will not be judged. Do not condemn, and you shall not be condemned. Pardon, and you shall be pardoned. Give, and it shall be given to you" (Luke 6:37-38). Once again, Jesus emphasizes that we can expect to be treated in the way we treat others. "For the measure you measure with will be measured back to you" (Luke 6:38).

Like all authentic virtues, compassion is rooted in the human mind and will. But more than some other virtues, compassion seeks an external outlet. Compassion expresses itself not only in attitudes and viewpoints but also in actions. When I was young, I had to memorize "the corporal and spiritual works of mercy." I'm glad I did because this catechetical tool summarizes a lot of biblical and Christian wisdom. The works of mercy are, in effect, concrete ways of making compassion real in our lives.

It may be worth recalling them here. The corporal works of mercy (see Matthew 25:31-40) may be stated thus: to feed the hungry; to give drink to the thirsty; to clothe the naked; to visit the imprisoned; to shelter the homeless; to visit the sick; to bury the dead. The spiritual works of mercy are: to admonish the sinner; to instruct the ignorant; to counsel the doubtful; to comfort the sorrowful; to bear wrongs patiently; to forgive all injuries; to pray for the living and the dead. If we are called to be compassionate as our heavenly Father is, these works of compassion or mercy will find a prominent place in our lives!

PRAYER: "Remember not against us the iniquities
                 of the past;
                 may your compassion quickly come
                 to us,
                 for we are brought very low" (Psalm 79:8).
PRACTICE: Today I will do a work of mercy *(name it)* for this
                 particular person *(name him or her)*.

41

TUESDAY, SECOND WEEK OF LENT
Scripture Readings: Isaiah 1:10-20
Matthew 23:1-12
"Whoever exalts himself shall be humbled, but whoever humbles himself shall be exalted" (Matthew 23:12).

HUMILITY

Jesus implies that humility is a positive virtue. Most people seem to think it is a negative virtue at best and, in truth, a handicap. While many persons seem to think of humility as a repressive virtue, Jesus indicates that it is, in fact, a liberating one.

It is not easy, of course, to summarize what the Gospel means by humility. The great Saint Theresa described it in one word: truth. That seems to be an excellent definition, provided we understand it. To do that we have to break it into two parts. Humility is truth, to be sure, but truth in self-knowledge and truth in action.

Truth in self-knowledge: This is the core of humility. It means that we have a real awareness of our human condition as creatures of God. It means that we do not lose sight of this most basic truth about ourselves: that God is our Creator and our loving Father. "For the God who made the world and all that is in it, the Lord of heaven and earth, does not dwell in sanctuaries made by human hands; nor does he receive man's service as if he were in need of it. Rather, it is he who gives to all life and breath and everything else. . . . In him we live and move and have our being . . . " (Acts 17:24-28).

The most basic truth about ourselves is that every gift and talent we have comes to us from God. Truth in self-knowledge demands only that we remember this. In other words, humility does not require that we deny the gifts and talents we have, only that we acknowledge where they came from. The theme song of the humble person is: "Who confers any distinction on you? Name something you have that you have not received. If, then, you have received it, why are you boasting as if it were your own?'' (1 Corinthians 4:7)

Truth in action: This means that our basic conviction about ourselves and our talents and abilities (as outlined above) colors our manner, our speech, our association with others. Our entire bearing communicates that whatever talents we have are gifts of God. That is the truth, and we are happy to live in accord with it! We do not, therefore, put on airs, belittle others, lord it over them. We do not have to. We know the truth, and the truth makes us free.

Freedom is indeed one of the fruits of humility. It frees us from the tyranny of false images, from the petty conflicts of jealousy and envy, from the empty struggle to be what we are not. Humility lets us be ourselves. With it there is no more crazy fear of being passed over or neglected, no more phony desire to be praised or singled out. If there were more humility, would there not be less fear and tension in our lives? fewer ulcers and fewer tranquilizers and fewer psychiatrists? Thomas Merton has written wisely: ''For a humble man is not afraid of failure. In fact, he is not afraid of anything, even of himself, since perfect humility implies confidence in the power of God, before Whom no other power has any meaning and for whom there is no such thing as an obstacle.''

Peace is also a fruit of humility. The humble person is spared a good deal of the turmoil and anxiety that rob so many people of peace. Peace has been aptly described as ''the tranquility of order.'' In other words, we know who we are and why we are here and what God has done for us! Such a conviction brings deep peace.

Jesus spoke of the humble when he spoke of the ''poor in spirit'' and the ''lowly'': those who recognized their need for God, their dependence on him. To them he promised happiness now and in the future (see Matthew 5:3). No wonder he invited his disciples to ''learn from me, for I am gentle and humble of heart. Your souls will find rest'' (Matthew 11:29).

PRAYER: "Jesus, meek and humble of heart,
                make our hearts like unto thine!" (Ancient
                Prayer)
PRACTICE: Today I will acknowledge with gratitude this gift
                (name it) of the Lord to me.

WEDNESDAY, SECOND WEEK OF LENT
Scripture Readings: Jeremiah 18:18-20
                           Matthew 20:17-28
**"Anyone among you who aspires to greatness must serve
the rest, and whoever wants to rank first among you must
serve the needs of all" (Matthew 20:26-27).**

AUTHORITY AS SERVICE

Thrust into some measure of authority over others (as parent,
teacher, office manager, coach . . .), most of us must sooner or
later experience the shattering of illusions. One of the first hard
facts we come up against is that some of our subjects don't pay
attention! The basic things we have taught, indeed, pounded
home, haven't been learned.

The Gospel of today highlights such an experience in the life of
Jesus. The "hour" of Jesus was drawing near. He was "going up
to Jerusalem" where "the Son of Man will be handed over to the
chief priests and scribes, who will condemn him to death. They
will turn him over to the Gentiles, to be made sport of and flogged
and crucified" (Matthew 20:18-19). Yet, even at this late hour, the
sons of Zebedee (James and John), and indeed the other apostles as
well, did not really understand what was about to happen.

Instead of hearing what Jesus had been saying, they had been listening to their own drummer. They were still enthralled with the popular belief that the Messiah would come in power and glory, that he (like a good politician) would ''take care of'' his faithful followers. James and John (with their mother acting as spokesperson) wanted to have ringside seats at the Messiah's royal tribunal (see Daniel 7:9-10). They wanted to be in on the action when the pagans would undergo judgment.

Like any teacher, Jesus realized that he had to go back to the basics. He had to emphasize what their discipleship really meant. James and John would be with him in his final hour, to be sure; but this would entail not power and glory and judgment but, rather, sharing in his ''cup of suffering.'' (According to Acts 12:2, James was beheaded by Herod Agrippa in A.D. 44. Though there is no explicit record of John's martyrdom, it is clear that he shared in the sufferings of Jesus.)

The other ten apostles ''were indignant'' at James and John. But they were indignant for the wrong reasons. In truth they, too, were deceived about Jesus' Messiahship. They were not indignant because they disagreed with the viewpoint of James and John; rather, they were indignant because they disagreed with the allocation of the best seats in the tribunal!

For all of his apostles, then, even at this late date, Jesus had to repeat a fundamental theme of his teaching. The idea of authority common at that time, the idea to which even his apostles clung, was that of absolute power, ''lording it over others.'' For the apostles and disciples of Jesus, however, it cannot be that way. ''Anyone among you who aspires to greatness must serve the rest, and whoever wants to rank first among you must serve the needs of all.'' The disciple must be like the Master ''who has come, not to be served by others, but to serve, and to give his own life as a ransom for the many.''

In a highly competitive and power-hungry culture like our own, this teaching of Jesus is extremely hard to put into practice. We are afraid that if we take it seriously people will laugh at us, take advantage of us, walk all over us. Yet, the teaching stands. As each of us exercises authority in his or her small part of the kingdom, we must act as servants not as secular lords.

PRAYER: "But my trust is in you, O LORD;
            I say, 'You are my God.'
            In your hands is my destiny; rescue me . . . ''
            (Psalm 31:15-16).
PRACTICE: Today I will exercise whatever authority is mine
            in the Christian spirit of service.

THURSDAY, SECOND WEEK OF LENT
Scripture Readings: Jeremiah 17:5-10
Luke 16:19-31
"Once there was a rich man who dressed in purple and linen and feasted splendidly every day" (Luke 16:19).

THE DANGER OF RICHES

The Gospel story today is about the rich man and the poor man Lazarus. In it Jesus speaks about one of his recurrent themes: the use of earthly riches. It is difficult to form a balanced view of the teaching of Jesus on material possessions. We run the risk of watering down some of his very hard sayings, on the one hand, or of reading into the Scriptures our own pet ideas, on the other hand. But since money plays a significant part in almost everyone's life, it is worthwhile to stand back, as it were, and take an honest look at what the Gospels say to us.

In the first place, Jesus did not condemn out of hand the possession and use of material goods. In the famous passage about the birds of the air and the lilies of the field, Jesus quite directly acknowledges our need of them (see Matthew 6:32). The urgent concern of Jesus was with the *attitude* of his listeners toward material goods. There is a danger that we can make them the be-all and end-all of our lives. ''Remember, where your treasure is, there your heart is also'' (Matthew 6:21). We can become slaves to money and all that money can buy. ''No man can serve two masters. . . . You cannot give yourself to God and money'' (Matthew 6:24).

In popular Jewish belief, at the time of Jesus, wealth was often considered a sign of God's favor. This is probably why the Pharisees were so fond of money and why Jesus spoke to them on the matter so frequently, as in today's Gospel. If you were good and righteous, the Pharisees seemed to believe, God would reward you by conferring wealth on you. Jesus exploded this myth. ''With difficulty will a rich man enter into the kingdom of God. . . . It is easier for a camel to pass through a needle's eye than for a rich man to enter the kingdom of God'' (Matthew 19:23-24).

Once again, the problem seems to be not money in itself but the illusion that somehow money makes a person morally good or independent of God and of others. ''Avoid greed in all its forms. A man may be wealthy, but his possessions do not guarantee him life'' (Luke 12:15). The rich man of today's Gospel ended up in ''the abode of the dead where he was in torment.'' The rich farmer who was so smug about his wealth and so self-centered about its use would hear God say: ''You fool! This very night your life shall be required of you. To whom will all this piled-up wealth of yours go?'' On this Jesus incisively comments: ''That is the way it works with the man who grows rich for himself instead of growing rich in the sight of God'' (Luke 12:20-21).

It is hard for the rich to enter the kingdom of God. But it is not impossible. The disciples (in the story of the rich young man) were aware that many of their contemporaries considered wealth a sign of God's favor. When Jesus denied this assumption, they concluded that practically no one could be saved. Jesus replied that it was possible for the rich to be saved if they, like the poor, recognized their dependence on God for salvation (see Matthew 19:16-26).

On balance, then, the teaching of Jesus seems to be concerned not so much with the good or bad of material things but with the attitudes, the values, the priorities of those who wish to follow him. The true disciple must know that it is not money that makes the world go round but freedom, trust, and, ultimately, love.

PRAYER: "Incline your ear, O LORD; answer me,
                   for I am afflicted and poor.
                Keep my life, for I am devoted to you;
                   save your servant who trusts in you" (Psalm 86:1-2).

PRACTICE: Today I will examine my material possessions in the light of the Gospel.

FRIDAY, SECOND WEEK OF LENT
Scripture Readings: Genesis 37:3-4,12-13,17-28
                              Matthew 21:33-43,45-46
"With that they seized him, dragged him outside the vineyard, and killed him" (Matthew 21:39).

JESUS, OUR BROTHER

The first reading today is a short excerpt from the long story of Joseph, as told in the Book of Genesis. The story itself is a miniature masterpiece, imaginative and interesting from beginning to end. Joseph, though the youngest brother, is a man of

48

wisdom and fear of the Lord; he is bighearted, always ready to forgive. He is "the ideal Israelite."

Biblically speaking, he is more. He is a "figure" or "type" of Christ. The parallels are striking: He is deeply loved by his father, but handed over to death by his brothers; his hopes of victory are fulfilled only after his suffering and humiliation; the evil done to him mysteriously brings deliverance for others. Shortly before his death, Joseph insightfully remarks to his repentant brothers: "Even though you meant harm to me, God meant it for good, to achieve his present end, the survival of many people" (Genesis 50:20).

As God drew "the survival of many" out of the afflictions of Joseph, so he would draw the salvation of many out of the Passion and death of Jesus. The parable of the wicked husbandman (today's Gospel) vividly points to this truth. Though some of the details of the parable are obscure, the main thrust is entirely clear. The vineyard symbolizes Israel; the owner is Yahweh God; the slaves are the prophets; the son is Jesus; the tenants are the religious leaders of Judaism. The vineyard will now be opened up to "foreigners," to the Gentiles, "to a nation that will yield a rich harvest."

Through the medium of this parable Jesus is predicting his suffering and death. There is a special poignancy to this prediction: It is made just a few days before the actual event; it is given in Jerusalem, the very city where his death will take place; it is spoken to the very people — the chief priests and scribes — who will have him put to death. By his saving death he will become "the keystone of the structure," the source of salvation.

As we reflect on the saga of Joseph, on the one hand, and Jesus, on the other, certain crucial lessons seem to emerge from the reflection. Perhaps the most important of these is that God can bring good out of evil, success out of failure, triumph out of defeat. Just as he brought deliverance and salvation out of their sufferings, so he will bring good out of the evils of our lives.

For this to happen, however, we must be ready, as were both Joseph and Jesus, to abandon ourselves into the hands of God. As long as we hold on to "human wisdom," refusing to accept the sufferings of our lives as redemptive, we place a serious obstacle in the way of God's plan for us. As we will emphasize in a later reflection, we must "let go and let God."

What is said here about evil and suffering in general applies with special force to the "evil" of death. In their commentary on Matthew's Gospel, Thierry Maertens and Jean Fisque offer this reflection: "It is only when man fails to put it in its proper context in the creaturely condition that death acquires strength. . . . If, after the example of Jesus, we confront it, its power is held in check, no longer does it have the last word in human existence. True, it does not disappear; but man becomes capable not only of loosening its grip, but of making it the springboard of a new existence, just because he accepts it in loving obedience. The stone that was rejected becomes the cornerstone" (*Guide for the Christian Assembly*).

PRAYER: "Into your hands I commend my spirit;
                 you will redeem me, O LORD, O
                 faithful God" (Psalm 31:6).

PRACTICE: Today I will feature a spirit of gratitude for all
                that God has done for me in Christ.

SATURDAY, SECOND WEEK OF LENT
Scripture Readings: Micah 7:14-15,18-20
Luke 15:1-3,11-32
"You will cast into the depths of the sea all our sins"
(Micah 7:19).

THE SHADOW OF GUILT

With a passionate voice the prophet Micah reproaches Israel for its sins. Like most of the prophets, he inveighs especially against those guilty of social injustice: the rich who exploit the poor; merchants who engage in fraud; corrupt judges, priests, and prophets.

"Woe to those who plan iniquity,
  and work out evil on their couches;
In the morning light they accomplish it
  when it lies within their power.
They covet fields, and seize them;
  houses, and they take them;
They cheat an owner of his house,
  a man of his inheritance" (Micah 2:1-2).

Unless they repent, Micah stresses, they can expect punishment from the Lord.

"Therefore you shall have night, not vision,
  darkness, not divination;
The sun shall go down upon the prophets,
  and the day shall be dark for them" (Micah 3:6).

Let Israel not forget, he repeats again and again, that sin deserves punishment.

Yet, at the same time that he reproaches Israel for its sins and describes the threat of punishment, the prophet also sounds a note of hope for forgiveness. In one of the most beautiful passages of the Scriptures, Micah says:

"Who is there like you, the God who removes guilt
  and pardons sin for the remnant of his inheritance;
Who does not persist in anger forever,
  but delights rather in clemency,
And will again have compassion on us,
  treading underfoot our guilt?
You will cast into the depths of the sea
  all our sins . . ." (Micah 7:18-19).

The word "guilt" appears a number of times in the preaching of Micah (and in the other prophets as well). It is a basic biblical concept. In our heavily psychological age there has been a tendency to remove "guilt" from the human condition. This tendency emerges from the conviction that guilt is unwholesome, neurotic, pointless. There is, in other words, a tendency to confuse true guilt and false guilt.

True (or real) guilt is a state or condition that follows upon a free, personal, deliberate transgression of God's law. Guilt, in other words, follows upon sin. Awareness of guilt gives rise to "guilt feelings" ("darkness," according to Micah) — that is, feelings of spiritual unrest or discomfort that seek relief. Guilt feelings, in their turn, urge the sinner to repent, to make amends, so that the feelings of guilt can be relieved. Micah spells out the familiar pattern: acknowledgment of sin before God, willingness to make restitution, forgiveness from a compassionate God, an experience of grace and renewal.

False (or neurotic) guilt arises not so much from deliberate, personal sin but from a generalized and compulsive conviction that "I am worthless," "I always do the wrong thing," "God cannot forgive me." Such convictions lead not to positive amendment and reconciliation but to progressive anxiety and unrest. Jewish and Catholic literature fairly bristle with sad tales of how religion created in young souls the torment of neurotic guilt.

True guilt is important. It is an objective fact. We are called, especially during Lent, to deal with it in an honest and constructive way. False guilt is tragic. Not only does it torment the soul of the person who suffers it but also cruelly hides the face of our clement and compassionate God.

PRAYER: ''You will cast into the depths of the sea
                  all our sins;
                You will show faithfulness to Jacob,
                  and grace to Abraham,
                As you have sworn to our fathers
                  from days of old'' (Micah 7:19-20).

PRACTICE: I will acknowledge my real sinfulness before the Lord and trust in his tender mercy.

THIRD SUNDAY OF LENT

Scripture Readings: Cycle A
                                         Exodus 17:3-7
                                         Romans 5:1-2,5-8
                                         John 4:5-42
                                       Reflection: LIVING WATER

Cycle B
   Exodus 20:1-17
   1 Corinthians 1:22-25
   John 2:13-25
Reflection: THE NEW TEMPLE

Cycle C
   Exodus 3:1-8,13-15
   1 Corinthians 10:1-7,10-12
   Luke 13:1-9
Reflection:
WHAT KIND OF GOD?

THIRD SUNDAY OF LENT
Scripture Readings: Cycle A
Exodus 17:3-7
Romans 5:1-2,5-8
John 4:5-42
"Everyone who drinks this water will be thirsty again. But whoever drinks the water I give him will never be thirsty . . . " (John 4:13).

LIVING WATER

One of the most charming scenes of the New Testament is the engaging encounter between Jesus and the Samaritan woman. It is a warm and touching scene, full of good humor and profound truth. It shows a very human side of Jesus; he is tired and hot and thirsty, yet still friendly and sympathetic to a woman he has never met before. It was unheard of for a rabbi to speak in a friendly way to a woman in public; it was almost a crime for a Jew to speak to a Samaritan and to request a drink of water from her. The Jews considered the Samaritans (and therefore their drinking utensils) "unclean."

Jesus pays little attention to the cultural barriers and the religious stereotypes. He encounters the woman at the well not in terms of nationality or sex or creed but in terms of her humanity, her inner spirit in need of healing and refreshment, her search for true fulfillment. It is evident that the woman, who is not exactly a model of moral perfection, somehow feels the warmth and wisdom of Jesus. She is not afraid of him; she opens her heart to him; she listens to him; she believes in him.

Jesus and the woman speak of many things. The pattern is that Jesus introduces a topic; the woman takes him literally; he then moves the topic into a higher realm of faith and revelation. "Give me a drink," he says. "You are a Jew. How can you ask me, a Samaritan and a woman for a drink?" "If only you recognized God's gift," Jesus replied, "and who it is that is asking you for a drink, you would have asked him instead, and he would have given you living water."

At first the woman takes "living water" to mean running water as opposed to well water, and she chides Jesus for pretending to know more than Jacob. But Jesus shows her that he is referring to "water of life," the water that will satisfy the thirst of the mind and heart and soul . . . and not just for an hour or two but forever. The words of Jesus echo the cry of Jeremiah:
"Two evils have my people done:
  they have forsaken me, the source of living waters;
They have dug themselves cisterns,
  broken cisterns, that hold no water" (Jeremiah 2:13).

For Jesus, "living water" means the Spirit, as John explains in a later section of his Gospel. "Here he was referring to the Spirit, whom those that come to believe in him were to receive" (John 7:39). It is not surprising, therefore, that the early Christians saw in the "living water" a reference to Baptism: the living water of Christ that gives the marvelous gift of the Spirit and the surpassing gift of eternal life.

Baptism, as the Church professes, is a new birth in water and the Holy Spirit. Baptism makes us the dwelling place of the most blessed Trinity, temples of the living God. Baptism makes us living members of the Body of Christ. And, not surprisingly, it brings with it serious responsibilities: to renounce Satan, to reject sin, to grow in faith, to love one another, to be witnesses of Christ in the world.

Lent calls us to a serious renewal of our baptismal promises. Are we dying to self? Are we rejecting the glamour of evil? Are we coming closer to Christ? Are we living the law of love? Are we giving witness to the Gospel? Lent is a time to meet Christ at the well, to be renewed in the living water of his Spirit!

PRAYER: "Lord, you are truly the Savior of the world; give me living water that I may never thirst again" (Verse before Gospel).

PRACTICE: Today I will renounce this evil in my life *(name it)* as a way of coming closer to Christ.

THIRD SUNDAY OF LENT
Scripture Readings: Cycle B
Exodus 20:1-17
1 Corinthians 1:22-25
John 2:13-25

" 'Destroy this temple,' was Jesus' answer, 'and in three days I will raise it up' " (John 2:19).

THE NEW TEMPLE

When I was in fifth grade, one of our scholarly pursuits was the study of Bible history. To be truthful, I do not remember much about the course as a whole, but I still remember the textbook used. Scattered throughout its pages were a number of classical paintings of biblical themes. One of the most intriguing, I thought, was "The Cleansing of the Temple."

Only much later did I discover that the painting was one of El Greco's. In the painting the figure of Jesus holds the central place. His eyes are flashing; his right hand, holding the "whip of cords," is poised to strike. All around him is pandemonium: tables falling over, merchants holding up their arms to protect themselves, bystanders aghast.

As strong and attractive as this painting is, however, it does not tell us much about the meaning of this event in the ministry of

Jesus. The meaning has certainly been variously interpreted over the centuries. Some people have pointed to this event as an indication of the "righteous anger" of Jesus. Others have seen in it a condemnation of "money-hungry pastors" who are always "talking money" and adding extra collections!

From a more biblical perspective, there are several complex levels of meaning in this event. One level centers on the Temple itself. The Temple was, of course, the center of worship in the religion of Israel. Various sacrificial animals were on sale at the Temple so that pilgrims would not have to bring them from a distance. Since Roman money was not acceptable at the Temple, the money-changers served a good purpose. The action of Jesus was not against this normal practice but against the formalism of the sacrifices offered in the Temple and against abuses (dishonesty, "robbery") which had apparently crept in (Mark 11:17).

But there is a far deeper meaning in this event. In effect, Jesus is announcing that the Temple is no longer the sign of God's presence but that he himself is the new Temple, the new dwelling place of the Father, the new *place* of sacrifice, the new source of blessings. " 'Destroy this temple,' was Jesus' answer, 'and in three days I will raise it up.' They retorted, 'This temple took forty-six years to build, and you are going to raise it up in three days!' Actually he was talking about the temple of his body'' (John 2:19-21). The body of the risen Christ is the new Temple!

It is clear that this deeper meaning of the action of Jesus has great significance for us Christians. First of all, our worship has value only insofar as it is united with the worship of the risen Christ: "Yet an hour is coming, and is already here, when authentic worshipers will worship the Father in Spirit and truth" (John 4:23). Worship "in truth" is worship according to the revelation of Jesus: "through him, with him, in him." Secondly, this worship finds its perfection in the Eucharist. For, as Leon-Dufour expresses it: "After his resurrection, this body of Christ, sign of the divine presence here below, will experience a new, transfigured state which will permit it to make itself present in all places and at all times in the eucharistic celebration'' (*Dictionary of Biblical Theology*). It is in the Eucharist that we become one with the Body of Christ!

PRAYER: ''How lovely is your dwelling place,
                    O LORD of hosts!
                    My soul yearns and pines
                       for the courts of the LORD.
                    My heart and my flesh
                       cry out for the living God'' (Psalm 84:2-3).

PRACTICE: During the remaining weeks of Lent I will try to renew and refresh my spirit of worship.

THIRD SUNDAY OF LENT
Scripture Readings: Cycle C
                    Exodus 3:1-8,13-15
                    1 Corinthians 10:1-7,10-12
                    Luke 13:1-9

'' 'I am the God of your father,' he continued, 'the God of Abraham, the God of Isaac, the God of Jacob' '' (Exodus 3:6).

WHAT KIND OF GOD?

How should we think about God? Should we think of him as the All-holy One, the remote and majestic Creator and Ruler of the universe, dwelling in inaccessible light? Or should we think of him as the Compassionate One, close to us, concerned about our needs, reaching out to us? In theological language, should we accentuate the transcendence of God or the imminence of God? Do we have to make a choice? Which image is "better"?

In a remarkable passage, the Book of Exodus (first reading for today's liturgy) deftly features *both* images of God. As Moses was tending his father-in-law's flock, he noticed a bush that was on fire but not consumed by the flames. As Moses approached the bush for a closer look, he heard the voice of God calling to him from the bush: "Come no nearer! Remove the sandals from your feet, for the place where you stand is holy ground" (Exodus 3:5). Not surprisingly, "Moses hid his face, for he was afraid to look at God" (Exodus 3:6).

In almost the same breath, however, God acknowledges that he has seen the sufferings of his people in Egypt and heard their cries of complaint. "Therefore I have come down to rescue them from the hands of the Egyptians and lead them out of that land into a good and spacious land, a land flowing with milk and honey . . . " (Exodus 3:8). He then delegates Moses to represent him before Pharaoh, and to lead his people out of Egypt.

Since Moses has not had the best of relations with Pharaoh, he desires to cover all questions. In those days, an envoy or delegate had no chance of being accepted unless he gave the name of the author of his mission. Bravely, therefore, Moses wants to know what he should say if they ask him God's name. "God replied, 'I am who am.' Then he added, 'This is what you shall tell the Israelites: I AM sent me to you' " (Exodus 3:14).

What we have in these passages is God's description of himself. Clearly, *no one image* can embrace it. No one theological word can adequately express it. He is, to be sure, the God of majesty and awe; he is the absolute and necessary Being, the Source of all created beings. Yet, he is also the One who tenderly listens to the cries of his people and breaks into human affairs to help them. (See also GOD WITH US under Wednesday of the Third Week of Lent). He is at once transcendent and imminent, distant and near, awesome and loving.

There is a subtle temptation, it seems to me, to get "locked in" to one or the other image of God. Many people seem unable to "go with the flow," to let God be who he is in all of his wonderful attributes, and to respond to him now in one way, now in another. The Eucharistic liturgy is most instructive here. We are called at one time to bow low in spirit and to sing to the transcendent God: "Holy, holy, holy Lord, God of power and might, heaven and earth are full of your glory." At another time we pray with trust and confidence to the imminent God that he will "give us this day our daily bread."

Far from trying to pin one and only one name on God, we should rejoice in the infinite attributes of his being. Far from striving to respond in one and only one way to the mystery of God, we should, like Moses, at one time hide our face from the splendor of his glory and at another speak to him from the troubled depths of our hearts.

PRAYER: "Bless the LORD, O my soul;
  and all my being, bless his holy name.
  Bless the LORD, O my soul,
  and forget not all his benefits" (Psalm 103:1-2).

PRACTICE: Today in prayer I will reflect on the "Holy, Holy, Holy" and on the "Our Father."

MONDAY, THIRD WEEK OF LENT
Scripture Readings: 2 Kings 5:1-15
Luke 4:24-30
"But his servants . . . said, 'if the prophet had told you to do something extraordinary, would you not have done it?' " (2 Kings 5:13)

GRACE IS EVERYWHERE

After frequently reading and reflecting upon the two Scripture texts for today's liturgy, I came to a conclusion which is not the main point of either text but perhaps hinted at in both.

Naaman comes across as "a big-time operator." Though afflicted with leprosy (a fairly common skin disease at the time), he was nonetheless a highly respected army commander. A young girl from the land of Israel urges Naaman to go to Elisha, the prophet, so that he can be cured of his leprosy. It is clear that Naaman was expecting an elaborate ritual. The prophet disappoints him. "Go and wash seven times in the Jordan, and your flesh will heal, and you will be clean."

Such simplistic advice irritates Naaman. He had made a tedious journey only to be told to wash in the muddied waters of the Jordan River. "Are not the rivers of Damascus, the Abana and the Pharphar, better than all the waters of Israel? Could I not wash in them and be cleansed?" As Naaman was about to return home, his servants reasoned with him: " . . . if the prophet had told you to do something extraordinary, would you not have done it?" Fortunately for himself, Naaman listens to the advice of his servants and does what he is told and is cured.

What seems especially interesting about this story is the fact that God accomplishes his purpose through simple people and in ordinary ways. The first suggestion for Naaman's cure came from a slave girl. The encouragement to do what the prophet recommended came from servants. The cure itself came from seven simple washings in the Jordan. No large, dramatic events! No special fanfare! God works in and through the simple things of life.

The Gospel of today's liturgy is taken from Luke's description of the very beginning of Jesus' ministry in Galilee. One of the points that Jesus makes is that his own people refused to accept him, refused to hear with faith the message he preached to them. In this context he reminds his listeners of the cure of the non-Jew Naaman. In like manner, the kingdom would be preached to so-called outsiders, because "no prophet gains acceptance in his native place" (Luke 4:24).

It seems that Jesus was too ordinary for the people of Nazareth. How could he possibly be the Messiah? "How is it that such miraculous deeds are accomplished by his hands? Is not this the carpenter, the son of Mary, a brother of James and Joses and Judas and Simon?" (Mark 6:2-3) It seems that the neighbors of Jesus already had their minds made up about how the Messiah would come and what spectacular deeds would come before him. They could not accept the fact that Jesus was from God because somehow he was too human, too ordinary, too unspectacular.

Do we not often act like Naaman? Do we not frequently behave like the neighbors of Jesus? God touches us through ordinary people — the people with whom we live and work — but somehow that isn't dramatic enough for us. God speaks his word to us through his modern prophets, through his priests, through his poor. But we keep looking for other, grander voices. We so easily forget that grace is everywhere!

PRAYER: "Send forth your light and your fidelity;
they shall lead me on
And bring me to your holy mountain,
to your dwelling-place" (Psalm 43:3).

PRACTICE: Today I will try to appreciate how God works in so many "ordinary" ways in my life.

TUESDAY, THIRD WEEK OF LENT
Scripture Readings: Daniel 3:25-43
Matthew 18:21-35
"Then Peter came up and asked him, 'Lord, when my brother wrongs me, how often must I forgive him?' " (Matthew 18:21)

FORGIVENESS

Once, with a group of fourth graders, I was discussing the conversation between Jesus and Peter about forgiveness (today's Gospel). A dark-haired boy kept waving his hand for attention, so I finally called on him. He went on to explain that he had worked out the math of seven times seventy and that the total was four hundred and ninety! All the kids agreed that that was a lot of forgiveness!

But (though I did not get into this with the fourth graders) even four hundred and ninety times wasn't enough for Jesus. The number seven, according to biblical scholarship, already implies a certain completeness, a certain limitlessness. The seventy times seven only strengthens this and caps it off. The basic message is that for a Christian there is no limit to forgiveness.

The entire chapter 18 of Matthew's Gospel is concerned with relationships among the members of God's family, the Church. As far as Matthew is concerned, a spirit of lovelessness, unforgiveness, coldness is incompatible with the Christian spirit. Generosity in forgiveness is an essential mark of the Christian. Without it the spirit of Christ fades and dies.

Through the power of a parable Jesus underlines the basic reason why our forgiveness must be without limit. The reason is that we have received such limitless forgiveness from God. The parable of the unforgiving official — a man who had himself experienced the extraordinary generosity of the king — shows how this "worthless wretch" did not appreciate what had been done for him and did not see his responsibility to forgive as he had been forgiven. Jesus ties up the meaning of the parable by stressing that our forgiveness by the Father is dependent on our willingness to forgive others "from the heart."

To be sure, this was not an isolated theme in the teaching of Jesus. He returns to it again and again. In teaching his disciples how to pray, he includes the plea: "and forgive us the wrong we have done as we forgive those who have wronged us"; and almost immediately after that petition, as if to highlight it, he says: "If you forgive the faults of others, your heavenly Father will forgive you yours. If you do not forgive others, neither will your Father forgive you" (Matthew 6:14-15; see also Mark 11:25).

I have sometimes imagined (there is no way of knowing) that Jesus dwelt so frequently on the topic of forgiveness precisely because he knew how hard it would be for his followers. So many people have not yet experienced the forgiveness of the Father. They carry heavy burdens of guilt, both real and imagined. Because they have never experienced forgiveness, they cannot easily forgive. So many others seem to feel that to forgive somehow diminishes them, somehow deprives them of the sweet taste of revenge, somehow makes them a loser in the power struggle of life.

What a surpassing Lenten grace it would be for us if we were to have a fresh experience of forgiveness! Really, that is what the sacrament of reconciliation can do for us. The confessor is a representative of the People of God whom we have offended by our sins. He stands ready to sign forth for us the forgiveness of the Father, as we open our hearts in forgiveness of those who have offended us. The sacrament is both an experience of being forgiven and of forgiving. Its fruit is peace. "Through the ministry of the Church may God grant you pardon and peace!"

PRAYER: "Lord, in your goodness, forgive our sins against the unity of your family, make us one in heart, one in spirit" (*Liturgy of the Hours*).

PRACTICE: Today I will prepare my soul for the Lord's special forgiveness in the sacrament of Penance.

WEDNESDAY, THIRD WEEK OF LENT
Scripture Readings: Deuteronomy 4:1,5-9
Matthew 5:17-19

"For what great nation is there that has gods so close to it as the LORD, our God, is to us whenever we call upon him?" (Deuteronomy 4:7)

GOD WITH US

In the early books of the Old Testament there is an ongoing dialogue about the relationship of God with his people. Is he a distant God, or a God who is near? The Book of Exodus stresses that human beings can see the glory of God as reflected in the wonders of creation, but cannot behold his "face," cannot see him as he is. Thus, Yahweh tells Moses: "But my face you cannot see, for no man sees me and still lives" (Exodus 33:20). There is an emphasis on the transcendence of God: He is far above and beyond the created beings he has fashioned.

Yet, there is another emphasis as well. It is reflected in the reading from Deuteronomy in today's liturgy. It emphasizes the nearness of God, his presence to his people. No other nation can boast that its gods are as near to it as Yahweh is to Israel! This teaching on the nearness of God was symbolized in a special way by "the ark of the covenant," a visible sign of God's presence in the midst of his people (see Deuteronomy 31:24-26).

The theology of "the God who is near" blossomed forth as the new covenant dawned. In the person of Jesus, God establishes an entirely new kind of presence with his people.

"The Word became flesh
and made his dwelling among us,
and we have seen his glory:
The glory of an only Son coming from the Father,
filled with enduring love" (John 1:14).

Jesus, "the reflection of the Father's glory, the exact representation of the Father's being," is Emmanuel, God-with-us (see Hebrews 1:3).

The presence of Jesus among us is a many-splendored thing. The *Constitution on the Liturgy* (in #7) expresses the faith of the Church about the presence of Christ in these words: "He is present in the Sacrifice of the Mass not only in the person of his minister . . . but especially in the eucharistic species. By his power he is present in the sacraments so that when anybody baptizes it is really Christ himself who baptizes. He is present in his word since it is he himself who speaks when the holy scriptures are read in the Church. Lastly, he is present when the Church prays and sings, for he has promised 'where two or three are gathered together in my name there am I in the midst of them' " (Matthew 18:20).

In truth, Jesus is constantly present to us, but we are not often enough aware of his presence. In the tradition of Christian spirituality, there are two practical suggestions that can help us be more aware of the Lord's presence in our lives. One of these is called "the spirit of recollection"; the other is called "a visit to the Blessed Sacrament."

By the spirit of recollection is meant an active awareness of the presence of the Lord in our daily lives. It entails pausing from time to time, amid our work and recreation, to acknowledge the presence of God in whom "we live and move and have our being" (Acts 17:28).

The hallowed practice of visiting the Blessed Sacrament in the course of the day is a beautiful way of consciously taking time out of our busy schedules to place ourselves in the presence of Jesus. For, as Saint Alphonsus Liguori points out in his world-famous *Visits to the Most Blessed Sacrament:* "Real friends want to be with each other every moment they can spare. Sometimes they spend entire days together. Christ's friends are that way too: being before the Blessed Sacrament is the great joy of their life."

PRAYER: "O God, you are my God whom I seek;
                  for you my flesh pines and my soul
                    thirsts. . . .
                 Thus have I gazed toward you in the
                  sanctuary
                  to see your power and your glory . . . " (Psalm
                  63:2-3).

PRACTICE: Today I will take some time out of my busy life to visit with the Lord, before the Blessed Sacrament if possible.

THURSDAY, THIRD WEEK OF LENT
Scripture Readings: Jeremiah 7:23-28
Luke 11:14-23
"They walked in the hardness of their evil hearts and turned their backs, not their faces, to me" (Jeremiah 7:24).

THE HEART OF SIN

The first reading of today's liturgy is from the great prophet Jeremiah. In context, Jeremiah is trying to warn the Israelites about certain abuses in their worship and religious practice. The key message of Jeremiah is that external practices and sacrifices have no value unless they are accompanied by a sincere devotion of the heart. It is a message which would be repeated by other prophets and by Jesus himself on more than one occasion.

Jeremiah is very concerned about the quality of the relationship between God and his people. He often emphasizes the fidelity of God to the covenant, while at the same time calling attention to the infidelity of the people. He is extremely sensitive to the meaning of sin. Up to his time most references to sin by the prophets seem to refer to individual actions, to the violation of particular statutes. Jeremiah implies that some of the people are in a "state" of sin. This refers not so much to what the Church would later call "original sin" but, rather, to the reality that true sin involves a fundamental attitude toward God, a fundamental turning away from him. Jeremiah expresses this in metaphoric language: "they walked in hardness of heart"; "they turned their backs, not their faces, to me"; "they have stiffened their necks."

Jeremiah considers "faithfulness" as the essential element of the covenant. God is always faithful, but these people are not. He drives home this point with a touch of hyperbole: "Faithfulness has disappeared; the word itself is banished from their speech." It is almost as if Jeremiah has given up all hope that these people would ever see the reality of sin and infidelity in their lives.

In every age, but especially in a postconciliar age such as ours, Christians must give their attention to sin. Some people would say that too many theologians of our age have all but banished the word sin from their speech. Yet, if one delves deeply into the reflections of some modern theologians, very often one sees an effort to understand sin in a more profound and truly personal way. Like Jeremiah, many theologians are trying to focus our attention not primarily on the acts of sin but on the "state of sin," the fundamental attitudes and options which dominate our spiritual lives.

To be sure, these fundamental attitudes are expressed through individual actions — such as murder, abortion, euthanasia, adultery, fraud, graft — but all of these emerge from the deep recesses of our minds and hearts. The American bishops have expressed it in this way: "Sin . . . is a spirit of selfishness rooted in our hearts and wills which wages war against God's plan for our fulfillment. It is rejection, either partial or total, of one's role as a child of God and a member of His people, a rejection of the spirit of sonship, love and life. We sin first in our hearts, although often our sins are expressed in outward acts and their consequences" (*To Live in Christ Jesus*).

Like Jeremiah, these modern prophets are calling us to take sin not less seriously but more seriously. They are calling us to get behind the facade of our moral lives and see the hardness of heart and the turning away from God really present there. Only when we have faced the reality of sin will we be ready for the reality of conversion: a turning of our faces, not our backs, to God.

PRAYER: "Come, let us bow down in worship;
let us kneel before the LORD who
made us.
For he is our God . . . " (Psalm 95:6).

PRACTICE: I will look deep into my heart today and try to discover the roots of one of my external sins.

FRIDAY, THIRD WEEK OF LENT
Scripture Readings: Hosea 14:2-10
Mark 12:28-34
"One of the scribes came up . . . and decided to ask him, 'Which is the first of all the commandments?' " (Mark 12:28)

THE LAW OF LOVE

Rabbis and teachers — and indeed all who took the law seriously — often discussed the relative importance of the many commandments of the Old Testament. They searched for the "parent" commandment, the source of all the others. This is a natural and healthy kind of search; Christians still do it on a regular basis. The temptation for the Israelites, as it is for Christians, was to get things out of perspective, to put a heavy emphasis on what was, in fact, of minor importance.

In answer to the question about the "first" or "greatest" commandment, Jesus quoted a passage from the Book of Deuteronomy, a passage that was familiar to the Jews since it served as part of their morning and night prayers. This passage sums up the whole Mosaic law and is the keynote of the Book of Deuteronomy. The command to love the Lord God was considered the most basic and all-embracing demand of the covenant. Since the Lord is one God, the human response of love should be one and undivided.

In addition, Jesus quoted from the Book of Leviticus: "You shall love your neighbor as yourself" (Leviticus 19:18). Here the word "neighbor" was restricted to one's fellow countrymen, probably including foreigners who resided among the Jews. Jesus calls this the "second commandment." He goes on to emphasize that if one is searching for the relative importance of the many commandments one need look no further: "There is no other commandment greater than these" (Mark 12:31).

It is clear that both of these commandments were central to the religion of Israel. In his preaching Jesus took this for granted. At the same time, however, he added certain very important nuances to the understanding of these commandments. First of all, as we gather from the presentations of Matthew and Luke, Jesus combined into a single moral principle the love of God and the love of neighbor. There is one virtue of charity, as Saint Thomas expresses it, with two objects: God and neighbor. In addition, Jesus clearly expanded the notion of "neighbor" to embrace not only one's countrymen but even one's enemies (see Luke 6:27-35).

It is important for us to reflect from time to time on our experience of trying to live the law of love. There is a constant temptation, it seems to me, to separate the love of God and the love of neighbor. To adore, praise, and thank God while remaining at conscious enmity with others is to violate the teaching of Jesus. On the other hand, "doing good" to others without recognition of the love and service due to God is to twist the teaching of Jesus. The challenge for all of us is to hold fast to the one law of love with its twofold dimension, not to neglect God in service of others and not to neglect others in service of God.

Not surprisingly, this challenge is easier to state on paper than to incarnate in life. It demands that we give up false ideas of piety, that we allow no false separation between liturgy and life, that we see our practice of charity toward others as an integral part of our service of God. As we reflect on our lives today, we especially want to spot any false separations of the one law Jesus insisted on: love of God and love of all our brothers and sisters.

PRAYER: "Merciful Father, fill our hearts with your love and keep us faithful to the gospel of Christ" (*Opening Prayer of Mass*).

PRACTICE: I will abstain from meat today, both as a sign of love for God and as a prayer for the needs of my brothers and sisters.

SATURDAY, THIRD WEEK OF LENT
Scripture Readings: Hosea 6:1-6
Luke 18:9-14
"He [Jesus] spoke this parable addressed to those who believed in their own self-righteousness while holding everyone else in contempt" (Luke 18:9).

THE POISON OF PRIDE

A parable is a short story with a message. As we know, Jesus often used parables to communicate his basic teachings. Some of his parables are quite complex; others appear extremely simple. One of the most simple and direct is the one featured in today's Gospel.

There are only two characters in this short story: the Pharisee and the publican (tax collector). The contrast between them is sharply drawn. The Pharisee was proud of his virtue and looked down on everyone else. The publican was aware of his sinfulness and begged for mercy. Jesus draws out two conclusions from the parable. The first conclusion is particular: The humble publican went home justified; the proud Pharisee did not. The second conclusion is general: "For everyone who exalts himself shall be humbled while he who humbles himself shall be exalted" (Luke 18:14).

Yet, as we reflect on this parable, we may find ourselves asking questions that challenge its very simplicity. Doesn't Jesus seem to be quite hard on the Pharisee? Wasn't he, all in all, a pretty good man? Is there something wrong with being faithful to prayer and fasting and justice? What was so great about the tax collector?

To grasp the deeper meaning of this parable, we must underline the word *self-righteous*. The Pharisees actually did observe a strict fast every Monday and Thursday; they actually did give a tenth of their income to the service of the Temple. Surely, fasting and tithing are not of themselves evil actions or repugnant to God. The problem is not with these good works but with the belief of the Pharisees that because they were perfect in these works of the law they were therefore justified in the sight of God. The Pharisee's prayer was a smug expression of gratitude that he was on the way to holiness and eternal life!

The incisive moral point of this parable, then, is in the contrast between two views of justification before God. The Pharisee believes he is justified because he has perfectly performed the works of the law. The publican realizes that he has no self-justification and has no choice but to throw himself on the mercy of God. His prayer is a cry of the heart, like that of the psalmist: "Have mercy on me, O God, in your goodness" (Psalm 51:3).

Thierry Maertens and Jean Fisque pointedly summarize the meaning of this parable in these words: "The parable contrasts the 'just man,' who thinks he can justify himself, with the man who can only obtain justice by confident faith in God . . . .So does it prepare the way for the Pauline doctrine of justification given by God to people who cannot justify themselves (see Romans 3:23-25, 4:4-8, 5:9-21). Justification in these terms is obtained by means of the cross of Christ . . . and the instrument is baptism" (*Guide for the Christian Assembly*).

Lent, as we have already reflected, is especially a time for renewing our faith in the saving death and Resurrection of Jesus and for renewing the covenant of our Baptism. It is a time for letting go of self-righteousness and false confidence in our own good works. It is a time for draining off the poison of pride, so that the redeeming love of Christ can possess us completely.

PRAYER: "For you are not pleased with sacrifices;
should I offer a holocaust, you would
not accept it.

My sacrifice, O God, is a contrite
  spirit;
a heart contrite and humbled, O
  God, you will not spurn" (Psalm 51:18-19).

PRACTICE: Today I will make my own the prayer of the publican.

FOURTH SUNDAY OF LENT

Scripture Readings: Cycle A
                          1 Samuel 16:1,6-7,10-13
                          Ephesians 5:8-14
                          John 9:1-41
                          Reflection:
                          FROM DARKNESS TO LIGHT

                          Cycle B
                          2 Chronicles 36:14-17,19-23
                          Ephesians 2:4-10
                          John 3:14-21
                          Reflection:
                          THE MISSION OF JESUS

                          Cycle C
                          Joshua 5:9,10-12
                          2 Corinthians 5:17-21
                          Luke 15:1-3,11-32
                          Reflection:
                          THE PRODIGAL FATHER

FOURTH SUNDAY OF LENT
Scripture Readings: Cycle A
                             Samuel 16:1,6-7,10-13
                             Ephesians 5:8-14
                             John 9:1-41
"I know this much: I was blind before; now I can see"
(John 9:25).

FROM DARKNESS TO LIGHT

In the story of the cure of the man born blind (as indeed in other parts of John's Gospel), the theme of darkness and light recurs in splendid fashion. John features an ongoing struggle between the powers of darkness (evil, sin) and Jesus who is the Light of the world. The theme is set forth at the very beginning of the Gospel: "Whatever came to be in him, found life, life for the light of men. The light shines on in darkness, a darkness that did not overcome it" (John 1:4-5).

The restoration of sight to the man born blind is one of the "signs" of John's Gospel. This means, in a manner of speaking, that a certain "sign language" is spoken. To understand what the Gospel is saying, we must look beyond the physical healing to a richer reality, symbolized by the sign. Physical sight was a sign of the spiritual enlightenment that allowed this man to move from a superficial recognition of Jesus to a clear vision of him as the Messiah and Lord. Moreover, while the blind man moves from darkness to light, the Jewish leaders involved move further away from the light (who is Christ) and into greater darkness.

Before actually working the miracle Jesus announces its meaning: "While I am in the world I am the light of the world" (John 9:5). This rings like an echo of what he had dramatically declared on a previous occasion: "I am the light of the world. No follower of mine shall ever walk in darkness; no, he shall possess the light of life" (John 8:12). As the sun lights up the road of the traveler, so Jesus lights up our way to the Father.

The early Christians saw in this miracle a sign of Baptism. The story describes Jesus making clay out of spittle and dirt and anointing the eyes of the blind man with it. Anointing was part of the baptismal rite from earliest times, and the use of spittle itself came into the rite for a period of time. Baptism represents our "miracle," our way of moving from darkness to the light of Christ. Paul (in the second reading of today's liturgy) expresses it this way: "There was a time when you were darkness, but now you are light in the Lord" (Ephesians 5:8).

The choice before each of us is whether to be children of light or children of darkness. "The man who walks in the dark does not know where he is going. While you have the light, keep faith in the light; thus you will become sons of light" (John 12:35-36). Our choice must reflect itself in our moral lives. "Light produces every kind of goodness and justice and truth . . . Take no part in vain deeds done in darkness; rather, condemn them" (Ephesians 5:9-10).

Lent is a baptismal season: a time of preparation for those to be baptized and a time of renewal for those who have been baptized. Lent calls us to admit courageously the works of darkness which have become part of our lives and, then, to submit them to the shining light of Christ's mercy and grace. The works of darkness take many twisted shapes in our lives: pride, envy, lust, greed. But Jesus, the Light of the world, can overcome these works of darkness in us. All we have to do is let the Light shine in!

PRAYER: "Even though I walk in the dark valley
                I fear no evil; for you are at my side
                With your rod and your staff
                that give me courage" (Psalm 23:3-4).

PRACTICE: Today I will take an honest inventory of the
                "works of darkness" which I see in myself.

FOURTH SUNDAY OF LENT
Scripture Readings: Cycle B
                              2 Chronicles 36:14-17,19-23
                              Ephesians 2:4-10
                              John 3:14-21
**"God did not send the Son into the world
to condemn the world,
but that the world might be saved through him" (John
  3:17).**

THE MISSION OF JESUS

A grouchy professor of mine taught me and other students (not without anger on our part) a very important lesson. "In my classroom," he used to say, "you must always ask the right question. If you ask the wrong question, you will get the wrong answer. Also, you should ask basic and essential questions. My time is too important for trivial questions."

I was thinking about this forthright gentleman as I reflected on the Scripture readings for today's liturgy. Lent would seem to be a good time to ask ourselves, by way of review, the right questions. And because it is so easy for us to get caught up in the fringe questions of our Christian lives, Lent is also a good time to ask ourselves the basic or essential questions.

In terms of John's Gospel, none are more basic than these: What is the "work" or the "mission" of Jesus? Why did he come? What did he do for us?

The "work" of Jesus is, in a word, our salvation. "God did not send the Son into the world to condemn the world, but that the world might be saved through him." Or, as today's second reading puts it, "God is rich in mercy; because of his great love for us he brought us to life with Christ when we were dead in sin. By this favor you were saved" (Ephesians 2:4-5).

The "mission" of Jesus is the exercise of redemptive love. "The Son of Man has not come to be served but to serve — to give his life in ransom for the many" (Mark 10:45).

"Love, then, consists in this:
not that we have loved God
but that he has loved us
and has sent his Son as an offering for our sins" (1 John 4:10).

Another way of describing what Jesus did for us is to recall the Catholic doctrine of atonement. Atonement (at-one-ment) refers to our reconciliation with God through the sacrificial death of Christ. According to Saint Anselm (a medieval theologian), there is a kind of syllogism involved here: Since sin is an infinite offence against God, no ordinary being could offer satisfaction to the Father for it. It was necessary that the God-Man, Jesus Christ, offer complete satisfaction for sin through his sacrificial death. In this way, the justice of God was satisfied and God and man were reconciled. For this reason John the Baptizer calls Jesus "the lamb of God who takes away the sin of the world" (John 1:29).

These "mighty deeds of God" demand a response from us: the response of faith. Otherwise, we are worthy not of salvation but of condemnation.

"Whoever believes in him avoids condemnation
but whoever does not believe is already condemned
for not believing in the name of God's only Son" (John 3:18). Commenting on this text, *The New American Bible* notes: "Jesus' coming provokes judgment; his purpose is to save, but some condemn themselves by turning from the light."

This Sunday at the Eucharistic liturgy we will once again make our profession of faith, proclaiming that "We believe in one Lord, Jesus Christ, the only Son of God . . . For us men and for our salvation he came down from heaven. . . . For our sake he was crucified under Pontius Pilate; he suffered, died, and was buried. On the third day he rose again in fulfillment of the Scriptures; he ascended into heaven and is seated at the right hand of the Father.

He will come again in glory to judge the living and the dead, and his kingdom will have no end.''

This Sunday let us break through the barriers of habit and routine and, from the depths of our hearts, proclaim our faith in Jesus, our Savior and Redeemer!

PRAYER: ''Lord, by your cross and resurrection
you have set us free.
You are the Savior of the world'' (*Memorial Acclamation*).

PRACTICE: Several times today I will renew my faith in Jesus, Lord and Savior.

FOURTH SUNDAY OF LENT
Scripture Readings: Cycle C
Joshua 5:9,10-12
2 Corinthians 5:17-21
Luke 15:1-3,11-32

''While he was still a long way off, his father caught sight of him and was deeply moved. He ran out to meet him, threw his arms around his neck, and kissed him'' (Luke 15:20).

THE PRODIGAL FATHER

I once heard a Methodist minister preach a moving sermon entitled ''The Prodigal Father.'' He admitted that the title was partially a gimmick — to attract attention to the well-known parable of Luke's Gospel. Yet, the preacher went on to explain that the title was also quite accurate. For, while the word "prodigal" describes the unrestrained sensuality and extravagant life-style of the younger son, it also describes the lavish, profuse, unlimited love of the father for his wayward boy.

As one reflects on this parable, it is quite natural to focus attention on the two sons. The younger son — the impulsive, immature, self-deluding sinner — is fairly easy for all of us, in one way or another, to relate to. In some shape or form, we have all been down that road. Nor is the attitude of the elder son — the dutiful but self-pitying fidelity — foreign to us. If he is, as Scripture scholars suggest, a symbol of the scribes and Pharisees, we know all too well that there is a touch of pharisaical resentment in even the best of us.

All things considered, however, the focus of the parable is best placed on the father. For, as Pope John Paul II points out in his marvelous commentary on this parable, "There is no doubt that in this simple but penetrating analogy the figure of the father reveals to us God as Father" and "enables us to understand exactly what the mercy of God consists in" (*Rich in Mercy*). Though we may be able to relate experientially to the younger and/or the elder son of this parable, we have had no experience (even if our relationship with our earthly father has been richly positive) of a father like this one!

One of the most beautiful touches of this parable is that the very remembrance of his father's love and kindness allows the younger son to have new hope. "The prodigal son," writes Elizabeth Goudge, "caught the scent of some remembered goodness, the fragrance of some garden at life's beginning and of someone who had walked with him there" (*A Book of Faith*). Like the Hound of Heaven, the father's love is pursuing the boy even before he realizes he is in trouble.

The greatness of the prodigal father comes not from some outside force or some inner compulsion but from the father's fidelity to himself. In the words of Pope John Paul II, "The father of the prodigal son is faithful to his fatherhood, faithful to the love that he had always lavished on his son." This faithful love — "the covenant love" of the Old Testament — is a love marked by forgiveness, generosity, and affection. It is a love without equal, and it defines our God.

Lent may be seen as a special time for us to lay ourselves open to that love. For, to quote Pope John Paul II again, "This love is able to reach down to every prodigal son, to every human misery, and above all to every moral misery, to sin. When this happens, the person who is the object of mercy does not feel humiliated, but rather found again and restored to value." May that feeling be ours today!

PRAYER: "Who is there like you, the God who
removes guilt
and pardons sin. . . .
Who does not persist in anger forever,
but delights rather in clemency,
And will again have compassion on us,
treading underfoot our guilt?" (Micah
7:18-19).

PRACTICE: Today I will set aside some time in which to appreciate anew the Father's love for me.

MONDAY, FOURTH WEEK OF LENT
Scripture Readings: Isaiah 65:17-21
John 4:43-54
"The man put his trust in the word Jesus spoke to him and started for home" (John 4:50).

LET GO, LET GOD

The theme of today's Gospel story is trust. The royal official "put his trust" in Jesus, even before there was any sign of a cure. Jesus demands this kind of trust (or faith) before ever working a miracle. His miracles, after all, are signs attesting to his mission and witnessing to the kingdom of God. If faith or trust is not present, his miracles would lose much of their true significance.

Trust is always risky. It entails a certain self-abandonment, a certain yielding of control, a certain blind leap. The Israelites found it hard (see the lament of Jesus in Luke 18:8); not all the Gentiles responded as fully as the royal official; even the disciples were slow to trust.

There is an oft-told story about a dedicated jogger. No matter where he was or how late the hour, he never missed jogging. While on a business trip one time, after a long day of meetings, he hurriedly changed into his jogging clothes and went running in the local park. It was growing dark, and he was unfamiliar with the terrain. Suddenly, he found himself falling over a kind of cliff or precipice. Below were rocks and tree stumps and trash. Fortunately, as he was falling, he was able to grab a clump of vines and hold on.

As he hung on for dear life, frightened and fatigued, he raised his eyes upward and cried, "Is there anyone up there?" A voice came back: "Yes, I am here; I am the Lord." "O please, Lord, I don't know what to do; tell me what to do." "Let go, and I will take care of you!'' A long pause . . . and then the jogger said: ''Is there anyone else up there?''

Trust is never easy. The trust which Jesus demands of us means letting go of our prejudices, our pretenses, our pride. It means placing our absolute confidence in the Lord, believing in his unconditional love for us, accepting his word that he will be faithful to his promises. It is the spirit that inspires us to say: ''Even though I walk in the dark valley I fear no evil; for you are at my side . . .'' (Psalm 23:4).

It is noteworthy, I believe, that almost every modern self-help group has seen enormous significance in the spirit of trust. The third step of Alcoholics Anonymous (which has been of such tremendous help to so many people) expresses it this way: ''We made a decision to turn our will and our lives over to the care of God as we understand him.'' Whatever our particular problem may be, this attitude is extremely important. The popular slogan, ''Let Go and Let God'' is, it seems to me, a shorthand way of describing the kind of trust Jesus expected of his followers.

All of us struggle with conflicts and problems in our lives: fear, doubt, loneliness, insecurity, restlessness, a sense of failure. There are usually certain steps we can take to deal with these problems and to grow through them to a deeper Christian spirit — and surely the Lord expects us to take such steps. But there are times when we feel helpless, powerless, defenseless. At such times, especially, must we place our trust in the Lord. We must indeed ''let go and let God.'' The jogger has probably learned by now that there is nobody else up there! He had to learn the hard way. Let's hope and pray we don't!

PRAYER: ''To you I lift up my soul,
                 O LORD, my God.
              In you I trust; let me not be put to
                 shame,

85

let not my enemies exalt over me'' (Psalm 25:1).

PRACTICE: Today I will pause several times to renew my absolute trust in the Lord.

TUESDAY, FOURTH WEEK OF LENT
Scripture Readings: Ezekiel 47:1-12
John 5:1-3,5-16
"Remember, now, you have been cured. Give up your sins so that something worse may not overtake you"
(John 5:14).

JESUS, SOURCE OF NEW LIFE

The final chapters of the Book of Ezekiel highlight the return of the glory of God to the community of Israel. The magnificent temple will be the hub of this renewed people. In the reading chosen for today's liturgy, the author describes a stream of water flowing east from beneath the threshold of the east gate of the sanctuary. The stream becomes a river flowing into the salty waters of the sea; the sea is made fresh. This image of life-giving and refreshing water emphasizes the dynamic presence of God among his people.

Life-giving and refreshing water is also featured in the Gospel story today. Bethesda, a word which means "house of flowing water," was a kind of "hot springs" or spa to which people went for relief from their illnesses and even for cures. Ancient peoples had great respect for water because they knew how precious it was and how scarce it could be. They knew, too, of its destructive force in the form of floods and storms. The people believed that the moving, bubbling waters of Bethesda had curative powers.

The Gospel story focuses on one man who has been sick for thirty-eight years. Because he is slow moving, he always arrives too late for the fresh movement of the waters. Even after so many years, however, he still has a desire and a hope to be cured. In an instant, Jesus fulfills his hope. By a word Jesus heals the man of his illness. This miracle is another "sign" in the Gospel of John: It is an event which reveals something about the person of Jesus.

What does it reveal about him? First of all, that he is the "new life-giver." He is able to do what the "old waters" could not do: He is able to bring life to his people. Secondly, Jesus speaks with the authority of God, and with that authority calls people to judgment. "Remember, now, you have been cured. Give up your sins so that something worse may not overtake you." The "something worse" seems to refer to the judgment of God. Thirdly, Jesus, who "was well aware of what was in man's heart" (John 2:25), unmasks the distorted values of those Jewish theologians who put the minute observance of the law before the demands of compassion and love.

Our first encounter with Jesus is in the life-giving waters of Baptism. In one of the blessings over the baptismal water the Church prays: "Make this water holy, Lord, so that all who are baptized into Christ's death and resurrection by this water may become more perfectly like your Son." Through Baptism Jesus becomes for us the source of new life. But with that new life comes also the responsibility to give up our sins, to walk worthy of the vocation to which we have been called in Christ. We, too, must be conscious of the judgment of God. Finally, we must allow our values to be measured by the Gospel; we are called to root out of our hearts all false ideals of morality and spirituality, however fond we may be of them.

Like catechumens preparing for Baptism, we are all called during the season of Lent to renew our faith in the life-giving waters of Christ, which have been poured out upon us, and to recommit ourselves to living by his word.

PRAYER: "God is our refuge and our strength,
an ever-present help in distress.
There is a stream whose runlets gladden the city of God,
the holy dwelling of the Most High" (Psalm 46:2,5).

PRACTICE: Today I will spend some time reflecting on the grace of my Baptism and renewing my baptismal promises.

WEDNESDAY, FOURTH WEEK OF LENT
Scripture Readings: Isaiah 49:8-15
John 5:17-30
" . . . I am not seeking my own will but the will of him who sent me" (John 5:30).

IN SEARCH OF GOD'S WILL

Saint Alphonsus Liguori was a man of many accomplishments: founder of the Redemptorists, bishop, Doctor of the Church. He wrote extensively on Catholic theology and the Christian life. Like a master artist, he returned to several basic themes in his writing and preaching. One of these themes is especially relevant for our reflection today.

The overriding preoccupation of Saint Alphonsus was the love of God. He emphasized two dimensions of this love: first, God's love for us and, then, our love for God. The message of much of his writing is simply this: See how much God has loved you! A typical line from the writing of Saint Alphonsus is this: "If the love of all persons, all angels, all saints were combined, they could not equal the smallest part of the love of God for you."

God's love was shown in the Incarnation, Passion, and death of Christ and, especially, in his Resurrection. It is the risen Lord whom we receive in the Eucharist. Saint Alphonsus, using external objects to lead us to deeper mysteries, urged us to meditate on "the crib, the cross and the sacrament." In this way, he felt, we would begin to catch a glimmer of God's surpassing love for us.

How can we respond to God's love? There are many ways, of course; but one of the main ways, in the view of Alphonsus, is the way of Jesus himself. Of himself Jesus said: "It is not to do my own will that I have come down from heaven, but to do the will of him who sent me" (John 6:38). "I judge as I hear, and my judgment is honest because I am not seeking my own will but the will of him who sent me" (John 5:30). Of his disciples Jesus said: " 'Who is my mother? Who are my brothers?' Then, extending his hand toward his disciples he said, 'There are my mother and my brothers. Whoever does the will of my heavenly Father is brother and sister and mother to me' " (Matthew 12:48-50).

In line with this Gospel principle, Saint Alphonsus developed a basic summary concerning our response to God: "All holiness consists in the love of God; but the love of God consists in conformity to the will of God; therefore, all holiness consists in conformity to the will of God." Vatican II expressed the same truth in this way: "The faithful should use the strength dealt out to them by Christ's gift, as that, following in his footsteps and conformed to his image, doing the will of God in everything, they may wholeheartedly devote themselves to the glory of God and to the service of their neighbor" (*The Church,* #40).

But how, we may wonder, is the will of God revealed to us? One way is through the Scriptures, the word of God. Another way is through the Church, which teaches in matters of faith and morals with the authority of God himself. The will of God is further manifested to us in the duties and responsibilities of our state in life. And, very concretely, it is seen in the particular circumstances of our lives here and now. ''The chief point lies in our embracing the will of God in all the things that befall us, not only when they are favorable, but when they are contrary to our desires. When things go well, even sinners find no difficulty in being in a state of uniformity to the divine will; but the saints are in uniformity also under circumstances which run counter to self-love. It is in this that the perfection of our love of God is shown'' (Saint Alphonsus).

For the follower of Christ, in other words, nothing happens by chance. Even the crosses in our lives are there for a purpose. It is NOW, in these concrete circumstances of my particular life, that I either will or will not do the will of God and so achieve holiness!

PRAYER: ''Then I said, 'As is written of me in the book, I have come to do your will, O God' '' (Hebrews 10:7).

PRACTICE: Today I will try to see this particular circumstance *(name it)* as God's will for me.

THURSDAY, FOURTH WEEK OF LENT
Scripture Readings: **Exodus 32:7-14**
John 5:31-47
"How can people like you believe,
when you accept praise from one another
yet do not seek the glory that comes from the One
  [God]?" (John 5:44)

THE QUALITY OF FAITH

In the verses chosen for today's Gospel reading, Jesus turns the attention of his listeners to the evidence for his repeated assertion that he comes from the Father and does only the works of the Father. In verses 31-40 he actually gives a list of witnesses that support his claim. Yet, these are presented not so much as separate and independent witnesses but, rather, as various aspects of the Father's witness.

The first witness is John the Baptizer. Since John was "a man sent from God," they should believe his testimony (though Jesus himself does not put much stock in any merely human testimony). The second witness to whom Jesus appeals is not an individual but his own works, his miracles. "These works which I perform testify on my behalf that the Father has sent me." The third witness is in truth the Father himself, but his testimony can be heard only in the depths of the human heart. As the evangelist has expressed it elsewhere:

"Do we not accept human testimony?
The testimony of God is much greater:
it is the testimony God has given
on his own Son's behalf.
Whoever believes in the Son of God
possesses that testimony within his heart" (1 John 5:9-10).

The fourth witness is the Sacred Scripture, which comes from God and speaks of God's plan.

The point that Jesus emphasizes is this: Even though all of this testimony is available, still these people would not believe in him! In harsh language, therefore, he condemns their disbelief (see verses 41-47). He condemns it because it is deliberate and sinful. It stems from their self-centeredness and their pride. They do not care about God's will but only about their own. '...And you do not have the love of God in your hearts.'' In rejecting Jesus, they reject the glory of God. Their honored hero Moses will also condemn them because they have refused to believe the one about whom he wrote.

Commenting on this passage, John Huckle and Paul Visokay write: ''The faith which Jesus demands involves more than trusting in him: Jesus rightfully expects them to dedicate themselves to him and to commit themselves to a way of life to which he calls them . . . Jesus views their present attitude towards him as the reflection of, the culmination of, a lifetime of infidelity to the covenant and to the Father, which has driven God's word and God's love from their inner selves. Their decision to reject Jesus exposes them for the unfaithful disciples of the Father they really are'' (*The Gospel According to John*, Volume I).

As we apply these thoughts to ourselves, do we not find that we, too, hold back from dedicating ourselves to the Lord and committing ourselves to his way of life? Faith can never be simply an intellectual assent to truths revealed by God (though it certainly includes that); it always demands a profound personal gift of ourselves to Jesus, a passionate commitment of our minds and hearts to him. Lent invites us to shed the chains that keep us back from this total commitment of faith. It is the time for us to truly accept him as Lord and Savior. It is the time for real discipleship.

PRAYER: "Why, O LORD, should your wrath blaze up against your own people? . . . Let your blazing

92

wrath die down; relent in punishing your people" (Exodus 32:11-12).

PRACTICE: Today I will renew my faithful commitment to the Lord, holding nothing back.

FRIDAY, FOURTH WEEK OF LENT
Scripture Readings: Wisdom 2:1,12-22
John 7:1-2,10,25-30

**"So you know me,
and you know my origins?
The truth is, I have not come of myself
I was sent by One who has the right to send,
and him you do not know" (John 7:28).**

THE MYSTERY OF JESUS

It was autumn. It was the time of the Feast of Booths (or Tabernacles), a harvest feast during which the people camped out, recalling the days when their ancestors lived in tents in the desert after the Exodus. At first, according to the Gospel of John, Jesus was not going to attend the feast "because some of the Jews were looking for a chance to kill him." Later, however, he decided to attend, "but as if in secret and not for all to see."

Chapter 7 of John's Gospel (it would be good to read it now in its entirety) offers a dramatic description of the charged atmosphere into which Jesus walked. There were lively debates between those who favored Jesus and those who despised him as a deceiver of the people. Jesus arrived determined to teach what he had been sent to teach, to reaffirm his origins, to propose himself as the source of life. At the same time, it is clear that Jesus was becoming more aware that his death and his return to the Father were drawing near.

It is fascinating to note, as William Barclay has pointed out (in his commentary on this section), how many different reactions to Jesus emerge during the celebration of the Feast of Booths. There is the casual, almost cynical, reaction of his relatives (John 7:1-5). There is the confused, timid reaction of many of the people. "Some maintained, 'He is a good man,' while others kept saying, 'Not at all — he is only misleading the crowd' " (John 7:12). There is the arrogant and hateful reaction of the Pharisees (see 7:47-49).

As we reflect upon these reactions, we may consider them foreign to ourselves, part of an historical moment which hardly concerns us. Yet, perhaps we should pause to question ourselves. Leonard Foley, O.F.M., gives us a lead: "But what would we have done if we were in that crowd in Jerusalem at the Feast of Booths? Would we have been with the headline-hunters, who smelled a plot to kill him, and eagerly pressed around to see what he would say? Would we have been with those who said, very quickly, that he couldn't be the Messiah since it was known that he came from Nazareth, whereas the real Messiah's origin would be unknown? Or would we have been with those who were open to the genuineness of Jesus, his evident sincerity and authentic teaching — and who were willing to follow him without knowing how it would all come out, with the danger of being hounded by the same authorities who were plotting against him?" (*Weekday Homily Helps,* 1983).

These imaginative questions press us to consider more actual ones. How real is Jesus to my daily life? How willing am I to endure misunderstanding and suffering because of my witness to him? How serious am I about his teaching? Are there Gospel challenges that I continue to look away from? Are there invitations to deeper relationship with him that I continue to ignore?

If Lent means anything, it means entering more fully into the mystery of Jesus. It is "an acceptable time" to challenge our tendency to intellectualize the person and explain away the message of the Lord. It is a time to slake our thirst at the fountain of him who said: "If anyone thirsts, let him come to me; let him drink who believes in me" (John 7:37).

PRAYER: "Lord, to whom shall we go? You have the words of eternal life. We have come to believe; we are convinced that you are God's holy one" (John 6:68-69).

PRACTICE: Today, in all my undertakings, I will try to be more aware of the presence of Jesus.

SATURDAY, FOURTH WEEK OF LENT
Scripture Readings: Jeremiah 11:18, 12:19-20
John 7:40-53
"You do not see any of the Sanhedrin believing in him, do you? Or the Pharisees? Only this lot, that knows nothing about the law — and they are lost anyway!" (John 7:48-49)

THE CALL TO HOLINESS

As at the beginning of the Feast of Booths, so at its closing there were mixed reactions to Jesus. There was the reaction of the crowd. Some said that Jesus must be the prophet Moses; others that he must be the Messiah. There was the reaction of the temple guard (simple and unsophisticated men): "No man ever spoke like that before." There was the reaction of the Pharisees (proud and self-serving men): In effect, the Pharisees were saying that only the ignorant and uneducated accepted Jesus. Finally, there was the reaction of Nicodemus: a timid defense of Jesus, a request that he at least be given a fair trial.

In these reactions we see a faint shadow of the reactions of our own time. There are still the proud and the self-serving who do not have time for Jesus, who are so concerned about themselves, their power and prestige, that they dismiss Jesus and his message. There are still the timid and the tentative who would vaguely like to accept Jesus and his Gospel but who are kept back by nameless fears and doubts. There are still "the ordinary people," "the motley crowd," who believe in Jesus and follow him. This is "the community of believers"; this is the Church!

To be a member of the Church means many things. But perhaps most of all it means that we are called to be saints! In a magnificent passage Vatican II declares: "Therefore all in the Church, whether they belong to the hierarchy or are cared for by it, are called to holiness, according to the apostle's saying: 'For this is the will of God, your sanctification' (1 Thessalonians 4:3; see Ephesians 1:4). This holiness of the Church is constantly shown in the fruits of grace which the Spirit produces in the faithful and so it must be; it is expressed in many ways by the individuals who, each in his own state of life, tend to the perfection of love, thus sanctifying others . . . " (*The Church*, 39).

This "perfection of love" is not simply a high-sounding ideal; it is a goal that is attainable, even by the motley crowd! "In order to reach this perfection the faithful should use the strength dealt out to them by Christ's gift, so that, following in his footsteps and conformed to his image, doing the will of God in everything, they may wholeheartedly devote themselves to the glory of God and to the service of their neighbor" (*The Church*, 40).

What keeps us back from this perfection of love? I often think that Graham Greene, at the end of his classic novel, *The Power and the Glory,* gives a good clue. The "whisky priest," who had been on the run from government officials for ten years, is now awaiting his execution. "Tears poured down his face: he was not at the moment afraid of damnation — even the fear of pain was in the background. He felt only an immense disappointment. . . . It seemed to him at that moment that it would have been quite easy to have been a saint. It would only have needed a little self-restraint and a little courage. He felt like someone who had missed happiness by seconds at an appointed place. He knew now at the end there was only one thing that counted — to be a saint."

Lent is surely the time for "a little self-restraint and a little courage" (or perhaps a lot!). Not for their own sakes but as helps to the perfection of love, as steps on the way to holiness!

PRAYER:　　"Lord, may the power of your holy gifts free us from sin and help us to please you in our daily lives" (*Prayer After Communion*).

PRACTICE:　Today I will heed the Lord's call to holiness by this practice of self-restraint *(name it),* or this act of Christian courage *(name it).*

FIFTH SUNDAY OF LENT

Scripture Readings: Cycle A
Ezekiel 37:12-14
Romans 8:8-11
John 11:1-45
Reflection:
THE PARADOX OF DEATH

Cycle B
Jeremiah 31:31-34
Hebrews 5:7-9
John 12:20-33
Reflection: DISCIPLESHIP

Cycle C
Isaiah 43:16-21
Philippians 3:8-14
John 8:1-11
Reflection:
THE SINFUL WOMAN

FIFTH SUNDAY OF LENT
Scripture Readings: Cycle A
Ezekiel 37:12-14
Romans 8:8-11
John 11:1-45

"I am the resurrection and the life:
whoever believes in me,
though he should die, will come to
life;
and whoever is alive and believes in
me
will never die" (John 11:25-26).

THE PARADOX OF DEATH

While the village church bell tolled, we laid my friend to rest. I had come to concelebrate the Mass of Christian burial and to say the prayers of farewell at the grave. As I stood there with the holy water sprinkler and prayerbook in my hands, I thought about death and the story of Lazarus which had been read at Mass (and which is featured in the Gospel for this fifth Sunday of Lent).

For a Christian to contemplate death is to come face to face with a paradox. Death is a sadness, yet a joy. Death is a loss, yet a gain. Death is an ending, yet a beginning.

The sadness of death stems from a fact of life: namely, that human life draws its richness and fullness from the quality of the human relationships which make it up. When a loved one dies, the human relationship — so vital, so precious — no longer exists in the same way. It comes to an end. And that is immeasurably sad. Yet, at the same time, as the early Christians liked to put it, there is joy because a pilgrim has "gone home to God." Without the leave-taking there could be no homecoming. Yet, homecoming is the ultimate meaning of Christian life.

The death of a loved one, no matter how long expected, always seems sudden and harsh. It is as if a beautiful flower were rudely plucked from the center of a garden, leaving only a gaping hole. But there is joy too. Did not Saint Paul announce in ringing terms: "For, to me, 'life' means Christ; hence dying is so much gain" (Philippians 1:21)? Perfect union with Christ is the ultimate joy. But it is possible only in the wake of death.

Death is an ending: The smile is gone; the laughter is silenced; the wisdom is stilled. In the words of Edna St. Vincent Millay, "The answers quick and keen, the honest look, the laughter, the love,/They are gone . . ." (*Dirge Without Music*). Yet, death is a beginning too: a bursting forth into that new and unending life with God, where "there shall be no more death or mourning, crying out or pain, for the former world has passed away" (Revelation 21:4).

Jesus experienced the sadness and the loss of death. He wept over the death of his friend Lazarus. He was gently sympathetic with Martha and Mary, the sisters of Lazarus, who were also his close friends. Only a strange kind of Christianity pretends that faith removes all feelings of grief and sadness. Yet, it was precisely in this context of sadness and loss that he pronounced his greatest promise — the promise of eternal life. Only God could do that. In his humanity Jesus experienced the sadness of death; in his divinity he changed that sadness to joy!

Life, for most of us, takes many unexpected twists and turns. We go through the cycle of emotions, from bright enthusiasm for life to a kind of dark desolation. The light that shines in the darkness is the light of Christ. The sound that echoes in the silence is the promise of Christ. It is so marvelous to know that death has no lasting power, that the victory of death is in truth no victory at all. "O death, where is your victory? O death, where is your sting?" (1 Corinthians 15:55)

Jesus asked one basic question of Martha. After issuing his great promise he asked: "Do you believe this?" Her unhesitating answer is, "Yes, Lord." It is the very answer that we in our turn give today.

PRAYER: "Yes, Lord . . . I have come to believe that you are the Messiah, the Son of God: he who is to come into the world" (John 11:27).

PRACTICE: Today, in a spirit of faith, I accept my death as God wills it, when he wills it, because he wills it.

FIFTH SUNDAY OF LENT
Scripture Readings: Cycle B
Jeremiah 31:31-34
Hebrews 5:7-9
John 12:20-33

**"I solemnly assure you,
unless the grain of wheat falls to the
   earth and dies,
it remains just a grain of wheat.
But if it dies,
it produces much fruit" (John 12:24).**

DISCIPLESHIP

The poignant picture of Jesus alone and fearful in the Garden of Gethsemani (see Matthew 26:36-45) is not retold in the Gospel of John. Yet, the same human hesitation and deeply felt fear is expressed in the passage chosen for today's Gospel reading. The decisive "hour" of Jesus was approaching. He had spoken of it often and knew the severe suffering that it would entail. He expresses his fearful struggle in one eloquent sentence: "My soul is troubled now."

Despite his fear and hesitation, however, Jesus remains faithful to the Father's will. He does not ask to be delivered from his hour but asks that the Father's will be glorified. ". . . yet what should I say — Father, save me from this hour? But it was for this that I came to this hour. Father, glorify your name! . . . " (John 12:27-28) This is an echo of Gethsemani's "your will be done." His passage through suffering and death to resurrection — his "being lifted up" — will be the ultimate glorification of the Father's name and the final victory over the powers of darkness.

As Jesus with deep emotion contemplates his death, his thoughts turn naturally to his disciples. As he so often did in the course of his relationship with them, he offers them now a frank, and even grim, appraisal of what their discipleship will mean. In a simple parable, borrowed from their familiarity with the good earth, he points to the paradox of "life through death." "I solemnly assure you, unless the grain of wheat falls to the earth and dies, it remains just a grain of wheat. But if it dies, it produces much fruit" (12:24). It is a paradox that would apply not only to him but also to them!

Lest the disciples somehow miss the point of the parable, Jesus explains its meaning in no uncertain terms: "The man who loves his life loses it, while the man who hates his life in this world preserves it to eternal life" (12:25). The disciple, like the Master, will have to experience the "life through death" paradox. As fullness of life would come through the Passion and death of Jesus, so the disciples would "produce much fruit" only by imitating him. Though life is the ultimate gift which the disciples will be asked to give (see John 15:13), it goes without saying that they will have to be ready to accept lesser sacrifices and hardships as well. They are called, in short, to serve Jesus with their entire lives.

This demand of discipleship is as real for us as it was for the first disciples of Jesus. In the familiar pattern now celebrated in Holy Week, Jesus heard the "Crucify him! Crucify him!" within a few days of hearing the "Hosanna to the Son of David!" Both represented for Jesus the Father's will. For the disciple of Jesus, too, sorrow will often be mixed with joy, suffering with achievement, dying with rising. But fidelity to the Father's will in good times and in bad will merit the final reward of discipleship: "If anyone serves me, him the Father will honor" (12:26).

PRAYER:　　"Father in heaven,
　　　　　　　the love of your Son led him to accept
　　　　　　　the suffering of the cross. . . .
　　　　　　　Help us to embrace the world you
　　　　　　　　have given us,
　　　　　　　that we may transform the darkness of its pain
　　　　　　　into the life and joy of Easter" (*Alternate Opening Prayer*).

PRACTICE:　Today, in the spirit of Jesus, I will avoid complaining about the suffering I experience.

FIFTH SUNDAY OF LENT
Scripture Readings: Cycle C
                            Isaiah 43:16-21
                            Philippians 3:8-14
                            John 8:1-11
"Jesus said, 'Nor do I condemn you. You may go. But from now on, avoid this sin' " (John 8:11).

THE SINFUL WOMAN

It is hard to find in the New Testament a more touching scene than the picture of the sinful woman standing face-to-face with the sinless Christ. Scripture scholars tell us that many of the details of this story are unclear, but surely the basic thrust of it is a living example of much of what Jesus preached.

Jesus had little patience with the legalism of the Pharisees. Here, in this passage from John, they are at it again! They set up the whole scene to trap Jesus "so that they could have something to accuse him of." Attempting to ensnare Jesus in one of the many traps of the law seemed to be a full-time job for the scribes and the Pharisees. They loved to put him in a no-win position. Here they wanted him either to reject the very strict Mosaic law or to give approval to adultery. It did not seem to bother them that they had dragged a young defenseless woman through the streets just to make a point.

Jesus challenged them at their softest spot. If only the sinless were allowed to judge, as they believed, were they willing to go on public record that they were without sin of any kind? Did their consciences pronounce them worthy to sit in judgment? Even the most arrogant of them did not want to go that far. And so one by one they began drifting away. They recognized that they had lost this particular confrontation with Jesus. They would wait for another day.

Jesus was then alone with the woman. He did not harangue her, make fun of her, condemn her. Kindly and gently, he actually extended to her the very same call with which he began his public ministry: repent, be converted, sin no more! In effect, he gave her a new lease on life. He showed her what compassion meant. He made her believe in the power of forgiveness.

I once heard a preacher say that he would never preach on this passage because it would give people the wrong idea. It would lead people to think, he said, that God condoned adultery and did not punish sin. And so this preacher, like countless so-called Christians before and after him, hid the compassionate face of Christ and made God in his own image and likeness. With great insight Pope John Paul II has said that "the present-day mentality, more perhaps than that of people in the past, seems opposed to a God of mercy and in fact tends to exclude from life and to remove from the human heart the very idea of mercy" (*Rich in Mercy*).

But this story is by no means an isolated example of Jesus reaching out to sinners: He had an uncomfortable way of going to their homes, eating with them, striking up a conversation at the well, meeting with them under cover of darkness. He spoke tirelessly of compassion, forgiveness, mercy. To quote Pope John Paul II again, "Christ confers on the whole of the Old Testament tradition about God's mercy a definitive meaning. Not only does he speak of it and explain it by the use of comparisons and parables, but above all he himself makes it incarnate and personifies it. He himself, in a certain sense, is mercy."

Would it not be a marvelous grace for us during this Lent to experience once again, and in a deeper way, the tender compassion and forgiveness of Christ? Perhaps we can have such an experience if we can give up the legalistic morality in which we take pride and stand humble and defenseless before the Sinless One, ready to receive his forgiveness, eager to repent and sin no more.

PRAYER: "Only goodness and kindness follow me
all the days of my life;
And I shall dwell in the house of the
LORD
for years to come" (Psalm 23:6).

PRACTICE: Today I want to hold myself open, in prayer and
life, to the absolute forgiveness of Jesus.

MONDAY, FIFTH WEEK OF LENT
Scripture Readings: Daniel 13:1-62
John 8:1-11

**"The whole assembly cried aloud, blessing God who
saves those that hope in him" (Daniel 13:60).**

THE STORY OF SUSANNA

The story of Susanna in the Old Testament Book of Daniel could
easily be turned into a made-for-TV movie. It has all the in-
gredients:

● Susanna: a young married woman, "very beautiful and God-
fearing."

● Two prominent, prestigious, but promiscuous older men who
lusted after Susanna (first separately, then as a team).

● Daniel: a handsome young man, wise beyond his years.

As the story unfolds, Susanna is with her maids in her private
garden and decides to bathe in the warm water of the garden's
pool. Meanwhile, two "elders of the people" who had been
appointed judges were hiding in the garden and spying on the
young woman.

In due time, they approached her and said: "Look, the garden
doors are shut, and no one can see us; give in to our desire, and lie

with us. If you refuse, we will testify against you that you dismissed your maids because a young man was here with you.'' Without hesitation and with beautiful fidelity to the Lord and to her husband, Susanna refused their lecherous advances, emphasizing that "it is better for me to fall into your power without guilt than to sin before the Lord."

True to their threats, the elders framed Susanna. Unfortunately, but not surprisingly, "the assembly believed them, since they were elders and judges of the people, and they condemned her to death."

Enter Daniel. "As she was being led to execution, God stirred up the spirit of a young boy named Daniel. . . . " He saw through the pretenses of the elders and showed how they testified falsely against her. By questioning them separately he caught them in their lies: "for by their own words Daniel convicted them of perjury." The assembly sentenced them to death.

The story concludes by noting that "innocent blood was spared that day" and "from that day on Daniel was greatly esteemed by the people."

Aside from its cinematic possibilities, what is the point of this story? The point can best be gleaned from the theme of the Book of Daniel as a whole. The book's overriding theme is that Yahweh is the Lord of history and that, despite the distress and persecution the Jewish people were experiencing, he would ultimately vindicate his faithful people. Written in a time of actual persecution (167-164 B.C.), the Book of Daniel offers comfort and hope in their time of severe trial. This general theme is made specific in the person of Susanna. In dramatic fashion, the story points out that God is just and will ultimately vindicate the innocent.

For the community of the Church and for the individual Christian, the lesson is still of fundamental importance. It is an apt reminder of the saying of Jesus:

"Blest are you when they insult you and persecute you and utter every kind of slander against you because of me.

Be glad and rejoice, for your reward is great in heaven; they persecuted the prophets before you in the very same way'' (Matthew 5:11-12).

The Church of our day certainly knows the taste of persecution. And so do we, as individuals, if we are trying to be faithful disciples of the Lord. The Book of Daniel, the story of Susanna, rings with a message of enduring worth: Our faithful God will see us through persecution and trial and will bring us to final victory.

PRAYER: ''O Most High, when I begin to fear,
               in you will I trust.
                 In God, in whose promise I glory,
                   in God I trust without fear;
                 what can flesh do against me?''
             (Psalm 56:3-5)

PRACTICE: Today, while being aware of this trial in my Christian life *(name it),* I will still renew my absolute trust in the Lord.

TUESDAY, FIFTH WEEK OF LENT
Scripture Readings: Numbers 21:4-9
                       John 8:21-30
"But with their patience worn out by the journey, the people complained against God and Moses. . . . " (Numbers 21:4-5).

THE DESERT AND THE CROSS

As with long lost cousins, there is a certain similarity between the two Scripture readings today, yet also a great dissimilarity. There is a ''sign'' involved here, a very important one, and it's crucial that we don't miss what it is saying to us.

The Israelites should not be judged too harshly, I suppose. Their journey was surely not an easy one: slow, hot, boring. They reacted quite naturally, with impatience and anger and rebellion. Yet, the impression lingers that they were a bit spoiled. Like children on a camping trip, they complained especially about the food! "Why have you brought us up from Egypt to die in this desert, where there is no food or water? We are disgusted with this wretched food!" (Numbers 21:5)

To speak in modern terms, it seems that by this time the Lord had "had it" with the complaining of the Israelites. In what appears an almost excessive reaction, he decides to punish them. He sent among them "saraph serpents" (a species of poisonous snake) "which bit the people so that many of them died."

The punishment was not lost on the Israelites. They owned up to their sinful complaining and asked Moses to intercede with the Lord for them. The Lord relented. To Moses he said: "Make a saraph and mount it on a pole, and if anyone who has been bitten looks at it, he will recover." Moses did as he was instructed. "Moses accordingly made a bronze serpent and mounted it on a pole, and whenever anyone who had been bitten by a serpent looked at the bronze serpent, he recovered" (Numbers 21:8-9).

In a remarkable passage the Gospel of John makes explicit reference to this desert incident. "Just as Moses lifted up the serpent in the desert, so must the Son of Man be lifted up, so that all who believe may have eternal life in him" (John 3:14-15). This "lifting up" of Jesus is, of course, a reference to his crucifixion, Resurrection, and Ascension. By his Cross and Resurrection he becomes the living sign of salvation to all who believe in him. The exaltation of Jesus, the I AM of the Father, brings to all believers the Father's healing and redeeming love.

As the bronze serpent was the "symbol of salvation" for the Israelites (see Wisdom 16:6), so Jesus is the ultimate symbol of salvation for us. Like the Israelites, in the desert of our lives we frequently complain about God's plan for us. We fall into a habit of self-pity: a habit of concentrating on our daily troubles and sorrows. We allow this negative pattern to alienate us from God, erode our relationships with others, cast a black shadow over our lives.

The first step for us, as for the Israelites, is to acknowledge that "we have sinned in complaining against the Lord." The second step is to look upon the exalted Savior, so that we can be healed.

As Lent moves toward Easter, are we becoming more and more aware of the mystery of Jesus in our lives? Are we focusing our minds and hearts once again on who Jesus is and what he has done for us? He is the Word made flesh, sent by the Father to all of us who wander in the desert. He comes to bring life to all who will open their hearts to his saving message. Lifted up on the Cross, he is in truth the supreme manifestation of the Father's love for us. The bronze serpent has given way to the living Savior!

PRAYER: "Keep in mind that Jesus Christ has died for us
And is risen from the dead.
He is our saving Lord,
He is joy for all ages" *(Lucien Deiss).*

PRACTICE: Today I will take time to contemplate the crucifix as a symbol of Christ's saving love.

WEDNESDAY, FIFTH WEEK OF LENT
Scripture Readings: Daniel 3:14-20,91-92,95
John 8:31-42
"I give you my assurance,
everyone who lives in sin
is the slave of sin" (John 8:34).

SLAVERY AND FREEDOM

In the winding course of Christian history, few subjects have
been discussed as often as sin. Christian people, reflecting on both
the Scriptures and their own moral experience, have searched out
the fundamental meaning of sin. The search has been conducted
differently in different generations, but the ultimate goal has
always been the same: What is sin? How shall we describe it? How
shall we deal with it in our personal lives and in society? Obviously, no one definition or description, no single image or meta-
phor, can capture the full meaning of sin. But the image used in
today's Gospel reading from John is particularly rich and instructive.

The image is that of slavery. Sin is slavery. Slavery as a social
institution was more familiar to the contemporaries of Jesus than it
is to us, but slavery in its basic meaning is not lost on our
generation. While the classical meaning of slavery involves some
measure of physical bondage and environmental limitation, the
more important dimension of slavery is spiritual. The real evil of
slavery is the loss of one's psychological freedom and moral
integrity. It is in that sense, especially, that sin is slavery. Saint
Paul distinguishes between the kind of slavery in which one freely
gives obedience to another and the kind in which one abjectly
submits oneself to a foreign power. Sin is the latter kind of slavery
(see Romans 6:15-23).

The person who is a slave to sin does not, in fact, do what he or she wants to do but what the power of sin wants to do. "What happens is that I do, not the good I will to do, but the evil I do not intend. But if I do what is against my will, it is not I who do it, but sin which dwells in me" (Romans 7:19-20). A habit of sin means that the grip of evil is so tight that one cannot, without supreme effort, shake it off. A person can allow a sinful attitude — pride, greed, lust, sloth — so to dominate him or her that it almost becomes part of his or her personality. Though various kinds of self-centeredness may, at first sight, seem harmless, they can gradually become the masters of the person who allowed them to get started. To allow oneself to be dominated by sin is to be a slave to sin.

The sinner-slave needs to be set free. In the same passage in which Jesus describes sin as slavery, he gives a clue as to how the sinner can find freedom. "If you live according to my teaching, you are truly my disciples; then you will know the truth and the truth will set you free" (John 8:31-32). True discipleship, in other words, brings with it the possession of truth; and truth in its turn makes a person free.

The truth is that the power of sin has been overcome by the power of Christ. Saint Paul explains that once sin reigned and we were slaves to sin, but now Christ reigns and we belong to him! And he concludes: "Now that you are freed from sin and have become slaves of God, your benefit is sanctification as you tend toward eternal life" (Romans 6:22).

In a manner of speaking, Lent is a "freedom journey." Freedom is never easily won. But it is worth the effort! In Lent we are involved in a journey to renewed discipleship and a fuller entering into the saving death and Resurrection of Christ. The journey is a hard one, for the chains that hold us in slavery are strong. But we do not make the journey alone. "If God is for us, who can be against us? Is it possible that he who did not spare his own Son but handed him over for the sake of us all will not grant us all things besides?" (Romans 8:31-32)

PRAYER: "I love you, O LORD, my strength,
              O LORD, my rock, my fortress, my
              deliverer" (Psalm 18:2).

PRACTICE: Today I will renounce something *(name it)* that
              keeps me from being truly free.

THURSDAY, FIFTH WEEK OF LENT
Scripture Readings: Genesis 17:3-9
John 8:51-59

"I will maintain my covenant with you and your descendants after you throughout the ages as an everlasting pact, to be your God and the God of your descendants after you. . . . On your part, you and your descendants after you must keep my covenant throughout the ages" (Genesis 17:7,9).

COVENANT LOVE

Though we do not use the word "covenant" very often in our ordinary conversation, we find that it holds a central place in our religious vocabulary. The word itself signifies a formal agreement, a contract. In religious terms it describes a very special relationship between Yahweh God and his people. Covenant is one of the key themes of both the Old and the New Testament.

Today's first reading describes some aspects of the covenant between God and Abraham. (For a fuller picture, start with chapter 15 of Genesis. Earlier in Genesis [6:18], the covenant with Noah is described. In chapters 5, 6, and 7 of Deuteronomy, the covenant with Moses is spelled out.)

In the covenant God formed a special agreement with his people, Israel. He promised to be their faithful God and to deliver them from evil. The people, in their turn, promised to be faithful to God, to worship him alone, and to keep his commandments. One of the dominant themes of the Old Testament is that while God is always faithful to his part of the covenant, the Israelites are, unfortunately, not always faithful to theirs.

The Hebrew word *hesed,* a word both mysterious and marvelous, describes the God of the covenant. Although biblical experts note how hard it is to translate this word into English, it includes such characteristics as loving-kindness, mercy, compassion, forgiveness. It is sometimes translated as "covenant love" or "covenant affection and loyalty." It comes close, I believe, to what contemporary theologians refer to as "unconditional love." God's dealings with Israel are always and everywhere marked with the sign of *hesed,* covenant love.

The new covenant does not annul the old but — in Jesus — brings it to fulfillment (see Galatians 3:15-29). The partners of the new covenant are God the Father, Jesus his beloved Son, and each Christian in and with Jesus. Jesus, the divine Son ("before Abraham was, I am"), now expresses covenant love for his people. He loves them unconditionally, instructs them, forgives them, and lays down his life for them. In so doing, he seals the new covenant in his blood. "This cup is the new covenant in my blood. Do this, whenever you drink it, in remembrance of me" (1 Corinthians 11:25).

Nor does the new covenant do away with the "old law" but, rather, brings it to perfection in the "law of love." When a lawyer, in an attempt to trip him up, asked which commandment of the law was the greatest, Jesus replied:
" 'You shall love the Lord your God
with your whole heart,
with your whole soul,
and with all your mind.'

This is the first and the greatest commandment. The second is like it:

'You shall love your neighbor as yourself.'

On these two commandments the whole law is based, and the prophets as well'' (Matthew 22:37-40).

Lent is a time for us to appreciate anew God's covenant love for us, manifested so beautifully in the saving death and Resurrection of Jesus. It is likewise a time for us to renew our fidelity in keeping our part of the new covenant. It is a time for worship of the true God, especially in the mystery of the Eucharist, and a time for loving one another as Christ has loved us.

PRAYER: ''Give thanks to the LORD, invoke his name;

make known among the nations his deeds . . .

Recall the wondrous deeds that he has wrought,

his portents, and the judgments he has uttered,

You descendants of Abraham, his servants'' (Psalm 105:1,5,6).

PRACTICE: During the remainder of Lent I will make a special effort to attend Mass daily.

Scripture Readings: Jeremiah 20:10-13
John 10:31-42
"If I do not perform my Father's works,
put no faith in me.
But if I do perform them,
even though you put no faith in me,
put faith in these works,
so as to realize what it means
that the Father is in me
and I in him" (John 10:37-38).

DOING THE FATHER'S WORKS

It was winter. The Feast of Dedication was underway in Jerusalem. (This feast was a celebration of the rededication of the altar and reconsecration of the temple in 164 B.C. after their violation by the Syrians.) Jesus was surely aware that his relations with the magistrates were deteriorating. His fate was taking a turn for the worse. As one reads John's Gospel at this point, one senses a certain urgency in Jesus' efforts to describe himself.

Jesus enters into a rabbinical dialogue with his enemies. There are subtle arguments and counter-arguments in this debate. In essence Jesus appeals to their experience of him, to the testimony of their own senses. He asks them if it is not true that he does the work of the Father. And if he does the work of the Father, does that not prove that he is one with the Father? "Indeed, just as the Father raises the dead and grants life, so the Son grants life to those whom he wishes" (John 5:21).

In the farewell discourse Jesus returns to this same self-description. In his reply to Philip's question, he says:
"Do you not believe that I am in the Father
and the Father is in me?

The words I speak are not spoken of myself;
it is the Father who lives in me accomplishing his works.
Believe me that I am in the Father
and the Father is in me,
or else, believe because of the works I do'' (John 14:10-11).
The marvelous works of Jesus, in other words, speak for themselves. Yet, only those who are seeking the truth will be able to see that "the Father is in me and I am in him." Those who were listening to him at the Feast of Dedication could not hear what he was saying or see what he was doing. They could hear only blasphemy. They wanted to arrest him.

Just as Jesus did the work of the Father, the Christian is called to do the work of Jesus! "I solemnly assure you, the man who has faith in me will do the works I do, and greater far than these" (John 14:12). The believing disciple will, in effect, continue the good work of Jesus in the world, not through any natural human power but because of the spirit of Jesus, the Paraclete, the spirit of truth, the Holy Spirit.
"I will ask the Father
and he will give you another Paraclete —
to be with you always:
the Spirit of truth,
whom the world cannot accept,
since it neither sees him nor recognizes him;
but you can recognize him
because he remains with you
and will be within you" (John 14:16-17).

Our Christian vocation, then, is to continue doing the work of the Father, the work of Jesus, in our own time and place. Saint James brings the meaning of this home to us: "My brothers, what good is it to profess faith without practicing it? Such faith has no power to save one, has it? If a brother or sister has nothing to wear and no food for the day, and you say to them, 'Good-bye and good luck! Keep warm and well fed,' but do not meet their bodily needs, what good is that? So it is with the faith that does nothing in practice. It is thoroughly lifeless" (James 2:14-17). There is no better time than Lent to put life back into our faith!

PRAYER: "Father, the hour has come!
Give glory to your Son
that your Son may give glory to you,
inasmuch as you have given him
     authority over all mankind,
that he may bestow eternal life on
those you gave him" (John 17:1-2).

PRACTICE: Today, in the spirit of Jesus, I will do a "good work" for *(name him or her)*.

SATURDAY, FIFTH WEEK OF LENT
**Scripture Readings: Ezekiel 37:21-28
                                      John 11:45-57**
"He withdrew instead to a town called Ephraim in the region near the desert, where he stayed with his disciples" (John 11:54).

THE SOLACE OF SOLITUDE

Jesus began his public ministry — his preaching, teaching, healing — only after a long period of prayer and penance in the desert. Now, as he comes toward the end of that ministry and closer to the ultimate ministry of his Passion and death, he returns to the desert. While the people were gathering in Jerusalem to prepare for the Passover feast, Jesus went with his disciples to the town of Ephraim, situated in the barren area north of Jerusalem.

We can have no doubt that Jesus "saw the handwriting on the

wall." The chief priests and the Pharisees were deeply afraid that if his popularity continued the Roman authorities would move in and straighten things out. And so "there was a plan afoot to kill him." Yet, for Jesus "the time had not yet come." The time would come only when he, not his enemies, freely decided. "The Father loves me for this: that I lay down my life to take it up again. No one takes it from me; I lay it down freely. I have power to lay it down, and I have power to take it up again. This command I received from my Father" (John 10:17-18).

In solitude and prayer Jesus summoned the courage to finish the work the Father had given him to do. Ahead of him lay the denial of Peter, the betrayal of Judas, the flight of his disciples, the agony in the garden, the scourging, the crucifixion. Now the desert would give him the time in which to recall and remember the Father's love, the atmosphere in which freely to give his ministry and life back into the Father's hands.

The example of Jesus must not be lost on us. We, too, need our "desert time," our time of silence and solitude, our time of inner renewal and refreshment. Without such time our faith becomes superficial, our courage sporadic, our love fragile. Such time is not a luxury but a kind of necessity. Surrounded by noise and distraction, we can gradually forget what our lives are all about, we can lose our connection with the Lord.

Silence has a way of restoring perspective and renewing depth. "For every one who wishes to hear what is true and real," writes Ladislaus Boros, S.J., "every voice must for once be still. Silence, however, is not merely the absence of speech. . . . It is a depth, a fullness, a peaceful flow of hidden life" (*God Is With Us*). Solitude provides the atmosphere in which we can remember all that the Lord has done for us in the past and experience all that he is doing for us now. In prayer and solitude we can face with courage the realities of our lives.

For most of us this "desert time" can be understood only in a metaphorical sense. We have many responsibilities and commitments: to spouse, to children, to students, to parishioners, to work, to community. But precisely because we have so many commitments, some "desert time" is crucially important. A period of time each day, or at least each week, should be worked into our schedule and kept sacred. We need a time and a place in which we can be silent, renewed, re-created. "Let there be a place somewhere," wrote Thomas Merton, "in which you can breathe naturally, quietly, and not have to take your breath in continuous short gasps. A place where your mind can be idle, and forget its concerns, descend into silence, and worship the Father in secret" (*New Seeds of Contemplation*).

PRAYER: "Jesus, Son of the living God, have mercy on me, a sinner."

PRACTICE: Today I will take some time in silence and solitude to unite myself to the Father's will.

PASSION (PALM) SUNDAY

Scripture Readings: Cycle A
Isaiah 50:4-7
Philippians 2:6-11
Matthew 26:14-66

Your attitude must be that of Christ:
he emptied himself
and took the form of a slave,
being born in the likeness of men." (Philippians 2:5,7)

PASSION (PALM) SUNDAY

Scripture Readings: **Cycle A**
Isaiah 50:4-7
Philippians 2:6-11
Matthew 26:14-66

Cycle B
Isaiah 50:4-7
Philippians 2:6-11
Mark 14:1-47

Cycle C
Isaiah 50:4-7
Philippians 2:6-11
Luke 22:14-56

Note: The following Reflection, THE PASCHAL MYSTERY, is suitable for Cycle A, B, or C.

PASSION (PALM) SUNDAY
Scripture Readings: Cycle A, B, C
"Your attitude must be that of Christ: . . .
he emptied himself
and took the form of a slave,
being born in the likeness of men" (Philippians 2:5,7).

THE PASCHAL MYSTERY

Today begins the celebration of Holy Week, the greatest week in the calendar of the Church. It is the greatest week because it celebrates the Good News: God has reconciled the world to himself in the suffering, death, and Resurrection of Jesus.

The great week begins with the moving liturgy of Passion (Palm) Sunday. On this day the Church calls to mind Christ's entrance into Jerusalem to accomplish his paschal mystery. In the words of the procession rite preceding today's Mass: "Today we come together to begin this solemn celebration in union with the whole Church throughout the world. Christ entered in triumph into his own city, to complete his work as our Messiah: to suffer, to die, to rise again."

The liturgy of this week is not merely an exercise in recalling past events. We share, here and now, in the saving mysteries of Christ. It is no exaggeration to say that our whole vocation as Christians is to share in the paschal mystery of Christ, to join with him in his self-emptying love. Let us briefly reflect on what this means.

In a magnificent passage Saint Paul states: "Continually we carry about in our bodies the dying of Jesus, so that in our bodies the life of Jesus may also be revealed. While we live we are constantly being delivered to death for Jesus' sake, so that the life of Jesus may be revealed in our mortal flesh" (2 Corinthians 4:10-11). Here Saint Paul teaches that in the mystery of Christ our lives take on new meaning. Our lives share in the dying and rising of Jesus — in the paschal mystery. Everything about our lives, the negative and the positive, is part of the death-Resurrection of Jesus.

The negative aspects of our lives take on new meaning: our day-to-day frustrations, our fears, our loneliness, our temptations, our failures — all of these are ways of sharing in the death of Christ. The positive aspects of our lives take on new meaning too: our joys, our health, our family, our friends, our successes — all of these are ways of sharing in the Resurrection of Christ. And so it is that every aspect of our lives — joys and sorrows, successes and failures — are joined to the life and experience of Christ!

It is not difficult to make a personal application of this great truth to our own lives. For example:

I DIE: When I am conscious of lifelong limitations in my-
          self . . .
          When I am tired, overworked, out of sorts, not
          feeling well . . .
          When I am discouraged by lack of success or of
          support . . .
          When I am fearful and anxious and worried.
I RISE: When I experience friendship and support from
          family and friends . . .
          When my talents and my gifts are recognized and
          used . . .
          When I feel joyful, happy, at peace . . .
          When Murphy's law fails and things go right!

Sharing more consciously in the paschal mystery of Christ is both a comforting and a challenging way to live. It means being able to say, all day, every day: "I wish to know Christ and the power flowing from his resurrection; likewise to know how to share in his sufferings by being formed into the pattern of his death" (Philippians 3:10).

PRAYER: "All glory, laud and honor
To Thee, Redeemer, King" (*Liturgical Hymn*).

PRACTICE: Today I will try to see everything in my life as a share in the dying and rising of Jesus.

MONDAY, HOLY WEEK
**Scripture Readings: Isaiah 42:1-7
John 12:1-11**
**"Here is my servant whom I uphold,
my chosen one with whom I am pleased . . . "** (Isaiah 42:1).

THE SUFFERING SERVANT

Six hundred years before Christ, the prophet Isaiah described in lilting language the Suffering Servant of God. His description takes the form of four religious songs or oracles. The Church uses parts of these four "servant songs" during this week of the Passion: on Monday, Isaiah 42:1-7; on Tuesday, Isaiah 49:1-6; on Wednesday, Isaiah 50:4-9; and on Friday, Isaiah 52:13—53:12. It would add greatly to our appreciation of Holy Week if we would seriously reflect upon these beautiful readings.

Biblicists interpret these songs in different ways, saying that they portray "the ideal Israel" dreamed of by Isaiah or the great leaders of Israel who were ideal servants of God: Abraham, Moses, Jeremiah, David, and others. But beyond doubt these songs also point to a new Servant who is to come, holier than any previous leader. That Servant, as the Gospel and the Church proclaim, is Jesus.

Jesus, the beloved Son of God, came "not to be served, but to serve," and said of himself, "I am in your midst as the one who serves you" (Luke 22:27). Jesus was sent to bring justice to the nations not through false power, violence, oppression but through mercy and compassion: "A bruised reed he shall not break, and a smoldering wick he shall not quench" (Isaiah 42:3). He came "to open the eyes of the blind, to bring out prisoners from confinement, and from the dungeon, those who live in darkness" (Isaiah 42:7). This redemptive work he would accomplish especially through his sufferings.

Abandoning himself to the will of the Father and offering himself in expiation for the sins of the world, "he was spurned and avoided by men, a man of suffering, accustomed to infirmity" (Isaiah 53:3). But by his suffering he became our Savior. "Yet it was our infirmities that he bore,

our sufferings that he endured . . . .

he was pierced for our offences,

crushed for our sins,

Upon him was the chastisement that makes us whole,

by his stripes we were healed" (Isaiah 53:4-5).

As we contemplate the sufferings of Jesus today, we are very much aware that his redeeming work must still continue in the world. The redemption continues now in his Church, the community of believers, the gathering of disciples. We, too, are called to be servants of God. We are called to make up for what is lacking in the sufferings of Christ.

The sufferings of our lives, as we have reflected often in these pages, take on a whole new meaning when they are united to the sufferings of Christ. In a mysterious way they become redemptive. The "apostolate of suffering," though not often publicized, is surely one of the most fruitful ministries in the Church. To suffer in union with Christ and in expiation for the sins of the world is to be his partner in death and also, therefore, in resurrection. "Do not be surprised, beloved, that a trial by fire is occurring in your midst. . . . Rejoice instead, in the measure that you share Christ's sufferings. When his glory is revealed, you will rejoice exultantly" (1 Peter 4:12-13).

PRAYER: "Into your hands I commend my
        spirit;
    you will redeem me, O LORD, O
    faithful God" (Psalm 31:6).

PRACTICE: I will today offer this suffering of mine *(name it)*
in union with the Suffering Servant, Jesus.

TUESDAY, HOLY WEEK
Scripture Readings: Isaiah 49:1-6
John 13:21-38

" 'Lord,' Peter said to him, 'why can I not follow you now? I will lay down my life for you!' " (John 13:37)

THE DIVIDED DISCIPLE

Of all the men and women who people the pages of the New Testament, Peter is one of the easiest to relate to. He comes across not as a "hero with a halo" but as a thoroughly down-to-earth human being. He was strong and weak, straightforward and ambiguous, arrogant and humble, selfish and generous. That is to say, he was, like most of us, a divided, inconstant person. As a simple fisherman, he must often have felt out of his depth as a disciple and as the first leader of the Christian community. He certainly had a lot to learn. The wonderful thing is that he learned it!

In the Gospel passage under consideration here, Peter picks up on what Jesus says about going away. In typical fashion Peter protests that he wants to go along with Jesus. In truth, Jesus seems to be speaking of his own death, and also of Peter's, when he says, "I am going where you cannot follow me now; later on you shall come after me'' (John 13:36). But Peter blusters on, asking why he cannot follow Jesus now. Peter is brave and forthright; he is not afraid (at the moment) of what lies ahead. ''I will lay down my life for you.'' Peter is not being coy, not trying to ingratiate himself to Jesus. He is being honest; he means what he says. The trouble is that Peter doesn't truly understand what is at stake.

Even as the death of Jesus draws near, Peter is still laboring under a momentous misunderstanding. He believes that he is capable, by his own will and strength, of following Jesus and of laying down his life for him. He has to learn, in the hard school of experience, that he trusts himself too much. Jesus knew that Peter was still weak, still wavering; and so he frankly tells Peter that a big fall is in store for him. As much as Peter loved Jesus, it must have been hard for him to believe that the predicted threefold denial would ever come about.

But come about it did. And it was the supreme moment of truth for Peter. He experienced the very depths of his weakness. He tasted the dry ashes of his own failure. Yet, in that very failure he finally learned that he could not, on his own strength, do what he wanted to do. Aware of his sin, Peter ''went out and began to weep bitterly'' (Matthew 26:75). The time would come when Peter would indeed lay down his life for Jesus, but by then he would know that this was possible only because Jesus had already laid down his life for him!

What Peter learned we all must learn. We cannot be faithful disciples of Jesus until we recognize our own weakness and rely entirely on his strength. Peter himself reminds us that ''the reason why Christ died for sins once for all . . . was that he might lead you to God'' (1 Peter 3:18). Our strength rests not in ourselves but in the Lord.

There is another lesson to be learned from this reflection on Peter. Many people, it seems, are genuinely scandalized by weakness and failure in members of the Church, especially so when those members are clergy or religious. Some people even leave the

Church on this account. It is important for us to admit that the Church is made up of sinners and saints. The glory of the Church, after all, is not in its members (though some of them are glorious) but, rather, in its head, the Lord Jesus Christ!

PRAYER: "For you are my hope, O Lord;
                    my trust, O God, from my youth.
                On you I depend from birth;
                    from my mother's womb you are my
                    strength" (Psalm 71:5-6).

PRACTICE: Today I will try to be more conscious of my
                absolute dependence on the Lord.

WEDNESDAY, HOLY WEEK
Scripture Readings: Isaiah 50:4-9
Matthew 26:14-25
"They paid him thirty pieces of silver and from that time on he kept looking for an opportunity to hand him over" (Matthew 26:15-16).

THE FAILED DISCIPLE

When I was quite young, I was told that the Wednesday of Holy Week was known as Spy Wednesday. From that time on Spy Wednesday has always had a distinct place in my mind, alongside Holy Thursday and Good Friday. I learned later that Spy Wednesday was not an official liturgical designation but one of popular origin. It is easy enough to see how people came up with the name. Judas "kept looking for a way to hand him over."

Judas Iscariot is the ultimate enigma. As Holy Week comes around each year it is only natural for us to seek more information about this man whose name has become synonymous with treachery and betrayal. We know for sure that Judas was "one of the twelve," especially chosen by Jesus to be his disciple. We have no reason to doubt that he received the same training as the other disciples. All four evangelists tell us that he was the betrayer of Jesus. Matthew tells us that he hanged himself.

Though the Gospel accounts indicate that the initiative to betray Jesus always comes from Judas, they do not offer us any clear understanding of his motivation. John's Gospel gives a clue that greed may have been the source of Judas' downfall. It was Judas (among others) who loudly complained when Mary anointed the feet of Jesus with costly perfume. "He did not say this out of concern for the poor, but because he was a thief. He held the purse, and used to help himself to what was deposited there" (John 12:6). It is clear, too (from verses 14 and 15), that Judas worked out a financial deal with the chief priests before agreeing to hand him over.

Jesus' condemnation of the act of Judas is about as severe as one could imagine. "The Son of Man is departing, as Scripture says of him, but woe to that man by whom the Son of Man is betrayed. Better for him if he had never been born" (Matthew 26:24). Yet, the Church has admonished preachers and teachers not to say that Judas (or any other individual person) is definitely in hell. Matthew does say that Judas experienced remorse or regret over his betrayal and flung the money back into the temple (see Matthew 27:3-8). Theologians and preachers have sometimes speculated that perhaps his remorse and regret did not come too late.

There is an interesting passage in Matthew's account of the Passover meal. "In the course of the meal he said, 'I assure you that one of you is about to betray me.' Distressed at this, they began to say to him one after another, 'Surely it is not I, Lord?' " (Matthew 26:21-22) Commenting on this, John L. McKenzie makes this remark: "That each of the disciples should ask seriously whether he was the traitor would exhibit a surprising insecurity, and this also points to a period of reflection when the Church came to realize that each of its members carries potential treachery within him" (*The Jerome Biblical Commentary*). Can not all of us say Amen to that?

In an old notebook I once jotted down a little verse by an anonymous author. It goes like this:

Still as of old, man by himself is priced;

For thirty pieces Judas sold himself, not Christ.

Perhaps that is the most basic lesson of Spy Wednesday. We have been called to be faithful disciples of the Lord. His grace is sufficient for our discipleship. To betray him is, in the most profound sense, to destroy ourselves.

PRAYER: " . . . at Jesus' name
every knee must bend
in the heavens, on the earth,
and under the earth,
and every tongue proclaim
to the glory of God the Father:
JESUS CHRIST IS LORD!" (Philippians 2:10-11)

PRACTICE: Today I will recommit myself in love and fidelity to the Lord.

HOLY THURSDAY
Scripture Readings: Exodus 12:1-8,11-14
1 Corinthians 11:23-26
John 13:1-15
"**What I just did was to give you an example:
as I have done, so you must do**" (John 13:15).

THE LORD'S COMMANDS

With the evening Mass of the Lord's Supper on this day, we begin the solemn Easter Triduum. Gratefully, we celebrate "the mystery of faith." Holy Thursday is sometimes called Maundy Thursday. Maundy refers to the "commands" which Jesus gave us. We might pause to recall and reflect upon these commands.

The first command of the Lord may be expressed thus: Take and eat! Take and drink! "During the meal, Jesus took bread, blessed it, broke it, and gave it to his disciples. 'Take this and eat it,' he said, 'this is my body.' Then he took a cup, gave thanks, and gave it to them. 'All of you must drink from it,' he said, 'for this is my blood, the blood of the covenant, to be poured out in behalf of many for the forgiveness of sins' " (Matthew 26:26-28).

The second command of Jesus is emphasized in the very institution of the Eucharist. "Do this in remembrance of me" (1 Corinthians 11:24). Paul here testifies to the faith of the early Christians and professes the faith of the Church.

From that time right to our own, as history testifies, the Church has never failed to come together to offer the Eucharist. The Church professes that the priest, through the sacrament of Holy Orders, "acts in the person of Christ in a special way." In the words of Vatican II: "Through the ministry of priests the spiritual sacrifice of the faithful is completed in union with the sacrifice of Christ the only mediator, which in the Eucharist is offered through the priests' hands in the name of the whole Church in an unbloody and sacramental manner until the Lord himself come" (*Priests,*

2). All of the faithful, moreover, are nourished by communion with the body and blood of Christ.

Holy Thursday celebrates with joy the institution of the Holy Eucharist and the sacrament of Holy Orders. We, the Church, rejoice that the commands of Jesus are still being fulfilled in our midst. Though unfaithful in many ways, we are yet privileged to stand in the long tradition of fidelity to his commands: Take and eat! Take and drink! Do this in remembrance of me!

The third command of Jesus is expressed by his dramatic and moving example of washing the feet of his disciples. "But if I washed your feet — I who am Teacher and Lord — then you must wash each other's feet. What I just did was to give you an example: as I have done, so you must do." The liturgy of Holy Thursday calls us to renew our commitment to the great law of love, the new commandment of Jesus to love one another as he has loved us!

These three commands of Christ are intimately related. The Eucharist is the outpouring of Christ's love upon us. Sharing in his sacrifice to the Father, uniting ourselves to him in Holy Communion, we are also united more closely with one another. Love is the fruit of the Eucharist. "Is not the cup of blessing we bless a sharing in the blood of Christ? And is not the bread we break a sharing in the body of Christ? Because the loaf of bread is one, we, many though we are, are one body, for we all partake of the one loaf" (1 Corinthians 10:16-17).

PRAYER: "Sing my tongue, the Savior's glory,
Of his flesh the mystery sing;
Of his blood all price exceeding,
Shed by our immortal king,
Destined for the world's redemption,
From a noble womb to spring" (*Liturgical Hymn*).

PRACTICE: Today I will attend the Mass of the Lord's Supper, if possible.

GOOD FRIDAY

Scripture Readings: **Isaiah 52:13-15, 53:1-12**
Hebrews 4:14-16, 5:7-9
John 18:1-40, 19:1-42

"Then he bowed his head, and delivered over his spirit"
(John 19:30).

THE DEATH OF JESUS

According to the ancient tradition of the Church, the Mass is not celebrated on Good Friday. The whole Christian world pauses on this day to recall the death of Jesus. The celebration of the Passion of the Lord begins with prayers and readings, with a special spotlight on the reading of the Passion according to John. After the readings and the prayers, there is the veneration of the Cross: "This is the wood of the cross on which hung the Savior of the world. Come, let us worship." Finally, there is a brief Communion service in which we receive the bread which was consecrated yesterday at the Mass of the Lord's Supper.

The death of Jesus was real. On the Cross Jesus gave up his life for us. He became our Savior. His death is a dramatic sign of God's overwhelming love for us. Through the centuries the crucifix has been embellished and decorated. There is a temptation to look away from the harsh reality of the death of Christ. There is a temptation to "prettify" it. Yet, it wasn't very pretty.

"There was in him no stately bearing to make us look at him. . . .
He was spurned and avoided by men,
 a man of suffering, accustomed to infirmity,
One of those from whom men hide their faces,
 spurned, and we held him in no esteem" (Isaiah 53:2-3).
 Why did he die?
"He was pierced for our offenses,
 crushed for our sins,

Upon him was the chastisement that makes us whole,
by his stripes we were healed'' (Isaiah 53:5).

''In his own body'' explains Saint Peter, ''he brought your sins to the cross, so that all of us, dead in sin, could live in accord with God's will. By his wounds you were healed'' (1 Peter 2:24).

The death of Jesus takes on personal meaning for us only when we recognize our desperate need of salvation. It is easy to think of sin in abstract terms or even in trivial terms. Only when we, like the saints, recognize the devastating power of sin in us, and our own powerlessness to be set free from it, are we able to grasp in an experiential way the meaning of ''Savior.''

Calvary signifies that in our desperate need God came to our rescue. ''It is precisely in this that God proves his love for us: that while we were still sinners, Christ died for us. Now that we have been justified by his blood, it is all the more certain that we shall be saved by him from God's wrath'' (Romans 5:8-9). The crucifixion is, in the phrase of Saint Alphonsus, ''a visible sign of God's passionate love for us.''

More than any other religious symbol, the crucifix demands a personal response from us. Dom Hubert Van Zeller, in *Approach to Calvary,* zeroes in on this fact: ''In the ordinary affairs of life we are bystanders, but on Calvary we are bystanders no longer. For good or ill we participate: we either let ourselves be caught up into Christ's act or else refuse to be identified with it. . . . If we refuse to join Christ in the final climax of his life, it means that we have never faced ourselves, never grasped the importance of sin, never understood about responsibility and guilt. If we accept the invitation, we come to see how inadequate we are, how corrupting sin is to us and what an outrage it is to God, how deeply we are involved in our own and other people's salvation or redemption.''

Though Good Friday was a sad and dark day for the disciples of Jesus, it is for us a good day: For we have been redeemed by the precious blood of Christ!

PRAYER: ''We worship you, Lord,
We venerate your cross
Through your cross you brought joy to the
world'' (*Liturgical Hymn*).

PRACTICE: My fast today will be offered as a visible sign of
my personal love of Christ.

HOLY SATURDAY
Scripture Readings: Romans 6:3-11
                    Matthew 28:1-10
**"If we have died with Christ, we believe that we are also
to live with him" (Romans 6:8).**

CHRIST: OUR LIGHT, OUR LIFE

The evening service of this day is called ''the mother of all holy
vigils.'' During the vigil we Christians, ''awake and watching and
holding lighted candles,'' greet the Lord with joy as he comes
forth from the tomb. The service of light reminds us that Christ is
the Light of the world, that in his Resurrection he triumphed over
darkness and evil. ''May the light of Christ, rising in glory, dispel
the darkness of our hearts and minds.''

Tomorrow the Church will sing: ''The Lord has indeed risen.
Alleluia!'' Easter is ''the most solemn of all feasts'' and for many
reasons. The Resurrection of Jesus is the Father's seal of approval
on the life and work of the Lord. In the Resurrection the Father
showed his acceptance of the maligned and crucified Messiah. By
it, God led into triumphant glory his only Son, who was ''obedi-
ently accepting even death, death on a cross!'' (Philippians 2:8)

The Resurrection of Christ is, moreover, the cornerstone of the
Christian faith. It was the central theme of apostolic preaching.

Paul proclaims the reason why: "If there is no resurrection of the dead, Christ himself has not been raised. And if Christ has not been raised, our preaching is void of content and your faith is empty too" (1 Corinthians 15:13-14).

The Resurrection of Christ is, in truth, the guarantee of our final resurrection, the source of all our hope. "If we have been united with him through likeness to his death, so shall we be through a like resurrection. This we know: our old self was crucified with him so that the sinful body might be destroyed and we might be slaves to sin no longer. . . . If we have died with Christ, we believe that we are also to live with him" (Romans 6:5-8).

Our incorporation into the death and Resurrection of Christ is brought about through Baptism — the Easter sacrament! The Easter vigil highlights Baptism. Catechumens are baptized during the vigil, and all of us are called upon to renew our baptismal promises. "Are you not aware that we who were baptized into Christ Jesus were baptized into his death? Through baptism into his death we were buried with him, so that, just as Christ was raised from the dead by the glory of the Father, we too might live a new life" (Romans 6:3-4).

As baptized Christians, then, we have a certain hope that we, too, shall rise glorious with Christ on the last day. This will indeed happen if we try to be faithful to the promises of our Baptism: "Since you have been raised up in company with Christ, set your heart on what pertains to higher realms. . . . Be intent on things above rather than on things of earth" (Colossians 3:1-2). It is in this context that Saint Paul also urges us to turn our backs on the sins we see in ourselves: anger, lust, pride and the like.

In addition to Baptism, we have another Easter sacrament: the Holy Eucharist. For in the Eucharist we receive "a pledge of future glory." In the Eucharist we receive the Christ who promised: "He who feeds on my flesh and drinks my blood has life eternal, and I will raise him up on the last day" (John 6:54).

We are a resurrection people, and alleluia is our song!

PRAYER: "Lord, by your cross and resurrection, you have set us free. You are the Savior of the world!" (*Memorial Acclamation*)

PRACTICE: Today with gratitude and love I will renew my baptismal promises.

EASTER SUNDAY

Scripture Readings: Cycle A, B, C

> Acts 10:34, 37-43
> 1 Corinthians 5:6-8
> John 20:1-9

"Let us celebrate the feast not with the old yeast, that of corruption and wickedness, but with the unleavened bread of sincerity and truth" (1 Corinthians 5:8).

EASTER LIVING

The Resurrection of Christ is, as we reflected yesterday, the cornerstone of our Christian faith. If Christ has not been raised from the dead, our faith will be empty indeed! (See 1 Corinthians 15:14.) But the Resurrection of Christ is not merely something "out there," not merely an historical fact at which we gaze admiringly. It is a present reality in which, through Baptism, we are intimately involved. "If we have been united with him through likeness to his death, so shall we be through a like resurrection" (Romans 6:5).

Our sharing in the crucifixion-Resurrection of Jesus brings about a mysterious change in our very being. Paul expresses it in a startling way: "I have been crucified with Christ, and the life I live now is not my own; Christ is living in me" (Galatians 2:20). The English poet Andrew Young, in his poem "Nicodemus," arrives at the same conclusion:

Why do I kneel before your empty tomb?
You are not here, for you are everywhere;
The grass, the trees, the air, the wind, the sky,
Nothing can now refuse to be your home;
Nor I. Lord, live in me and I shall live.

This intimate union between Christ and the Christian calls for a new way of life. We must change our behavior. Saint Paul writes that we should put to death whatever in our nature is rooted in earth (see Colossians 3:5), precisely BECAUSE we share the new life of Christ. Corruption and wickedness must yield to sincerity and truth. Commenting on Paul's perspective (today's second reading), Francis X. Cleary, S.J., insightfully remarks: "This reading serves as a healthy goad to Christians celebrating Easter Sunday. Much more is called for than external festivity. Christ has indeed risen, but spiritually we're behind the times, comfortable with daily moral compromises, our selfishness and little cruelties. Paul tells us to get going and make concrete changes so that our lives become characterized by sincerity and truth. He invites us to put teeth into today's annual renewal of baptismal promises." (*Scriptural Backgrounds,* 1983)

Putting teeth into our baptismal promises will challenge each of us in different ways. The goal is "Easter living" all year long. The means to the goal may vary, of course, but one practical approach, enthusiastically supported by many of the great saints, is the daily (or at least frequent) "examination of conscience." Far from being a nit-picking exercise in false guilt, this approach to "Easter living" is a practical way of renewing our motivation for such living and of bringing our baptismal promises into the nitty-gritty of daily life. A positive and consistent use of this means is a great help in overcoming, on the one hand, a mere legalistic approach to the Christian life, and on the other, a too ethereal approach.

PRAYER: "God our Father . . .
Let our celebration today
raise us up and renew our lives
by the Spirit that is within us"
(Opening Prayer).

PRACTICE: I will give serious thought today to the place a regular examination of conscience might have in my life.

SOLEMNITY OF THE ANNUNCIATION (March 25)
Scripture Readings: Isaiah 7:10-14
                                    Hebrews 10:4-10
                                    Luke 1:26-38
"Rejoice, O highly favored daughter! The Lord is with you. Blessed are you among women" (Luke 1:28).

HAIL, MARY!

The feast celebrated today is primarily a feast of the Lord. Its official title is "The Annunciation of the Lord." It recalls the beginning of God's plan of salvation in Christ. It is a reminder of the designated time when "God sent forth his Son born of a woman, born under the law, to deliver from the law those who were subjected to it, so that we might receive our status as adopted sons" (Galatians 4:4-5).

In this context of salvation history, the marvelous details of the incarnation of the Son of God are carefully described by the Gospel of Luke. Central to his description is the role of the Virgin Mary, who is a living sign of God's salvific plan as expressed by Isaiah (first reading today): "Therefore the Lord himself will give you this sign: the virgin shall be with child, and bear a son, and shall name him Immanuel" (Isaiah 7:14).

With the touch of an artist, Saint Luke describes the intimate dialogue between the angel Gabriel and Mary. The angel opens the dialogue with a special greeting: "Rejoice, O highly favored daughter!" This greeting signifies that Mary is the object of God's special favor and blessing, that she is "full of grace," that God has especially chosen and prepared Mary.

The angel then goes on to confirm that Mary has been especially chosen by God to bring to the world the fulfillment of God's promise — the Messiah — and to describe the Child whom she is to conceive. "You shall conceive and bear a son and give him the name Jesus. Great will be his dignity and he will be called Son of the Most High. The Lord will give him the throne of David, his father. He will rule over the house of Jacob forever, and his reign will be without end.''

"Blest are you among women.'' This greeting, spoken both by the angel Gabriel and by Mary's cousin Elizabeth, is also a shorthand acknowledgment that God's full favor has been shining on Mary for a long time and preparing her for the unique role she was called upon to play: a role expressed in Elizabeth's further acclamation: "Blest is the fruit of your womb.''

As we celebrate the Solemnity of the Annunciation, the wonders described in the Gospel demand a response from us. Perhaps this response can best be expressed in the ancient prayer of Christians:

Holy Mary, Mother of God: In words similar to those of the angel, we, too, greet Mary. We sum up all of her wonderful blessings from God by calling her "holy.'' We also pray to her as "Mother of God,'' recalling the doctrine of faith as expressed by the Council of Ephesus A.D. 431, that she is truly *theotokos* or God-Bearer.

Pray for us sinners: Here we acknowledge two basic truths about ourselves: first, that we are sinners, that we often fall short of what God has called us to be; second, that we need the help of God's grace. In light of these truths, we ask Mary to pray for us that we may be worthy of the promises of Christ!

Now: We pray for the help we need from God at this particular time in our lives, this NOW. We ask for the grace we need to fulfill God's will for us.

And at the hour of our death: We pray that Mary will especially intercede for us at that decisive moment called death, which is not an ending but a beginning of new life in Christ!

PRAYER: "Gentle woman, quiet light,
Morning star, so strong and bright,
Gentle mother, peaceful dove,
Teach me wisdom, teach me love" (Hymn by
Carey Landry, *Glory and Praise, I*).

PRACTICE: Today I will try to imitate the openness of Mary
to the saving will of God in my life.